Tyranny and Legitimacy

Tyranny and Legitimacy

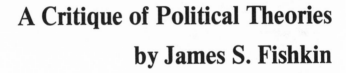

A Critique of Political Theories
by James S. Fishkin

The Johns Hopkins University Press
Baltimore and London

This book has been brought to publication with the generous assistance of the Andrew W. Mellon Foundation.

Copyright © 1979 by The Johns Hopkins University Press

Manufactured in the United States of America

The Johns Hopkins University Press, Baltimore, Maryland 21218
The Johns Hopkins Press Ltd., London

Library of Congress Catalog Number 79-11177
ISBN 0-8018-2206-8
ISBN 0-8018-2256-4 (pbk.)
Library of Congress Cataloging in Publication data will be found on the last printed page of this book.

To my mother and to the memory of my father

Contents

Acknowledgments

This is an expanded and revised version of my contribution to the fifth volume of *Philosophy, Politics and Society*. I would like to thank Peter Laslett for inviting me to join him as co-editor of that volume and for providing me with the occasion that initially prompted this essay. I would also like to thank him for many wise suggestions about my early drafts — suggestions I have incorporated into this longer version.

Five other political theorists have greatly influenced the development of this argument from the beginning: Brian Barry, Robert A. Dahl, Douglas W. Rae, John Rawls, and Bernard Williams. My debts to them should be clear from the essay that follows. My thanks cannot be adequately expressed here.

I would like to thank the Institution for Social and Policy Studies, and its director, C. E. Lindblom, for providing an environment that is as educational for its faculty as it is for its students. I would also like to thank the ISPS faculty seminar on American Democratic Institutions for helpful reactions to several presentations of this essay.

I would particularly like to thank Bruce Ackerman, C. E. Lindblom and Adina Schwartz for their comments on the final draft. Others who provided helpful comments on drafts at various stages include: David Braybooke, James Douglas, David Fishkin, Ronald Jager, Evan Kwerel, Joseph La Palombara, David Mayhew, Jonathan Mendilow, Thomas Morowitz, Ronald Rogowski, and Susan Rose-Ackerman.

David Colesworthy patiently typed several versions of this manuscript. I would particularly like to thank him for his editorial suggestions.

Lastly, I would like to thank my father-in-law, Milton Fisher, for providing wisdom and shrewd advice, and I would like to thank my wife, Shelley, for providing help in innumerable ways.

Part One. A Principle of Nontyranny

1. Introduction

Imagine a moral principle invoked by a government to justify its policies. Let's call this principle "X." If the government applies principle X without exceptions or qualifications, it would force people to starve when there was no need for them to starve. It would destroy lives needlessly, imprison people arbitrarily, and impose gratuitously deprivations so severe as to make life a constant ache of misery. X would support all of these results—even when there were alternative policies that would not have imposed *any* such deprivations.

In this book I argue that virtually all of the principles currently prominent in political theory have the properties of principle X: If applied without exceptions or qualifications, they would all legitimate acts by the government imposing severe deprivations when those deprivations were entirely avoidable. If applied without exceptions or qualifications, all of these principles would legitimate what is defined here as "tyranny."

Proponents of the principles I discuss may respond by explaining that their principles were never meant to apply to the examples I cite. In some cases this may well be correct. But once exceptions or qualifications (designed to rule out nasty counterexamples) are *explicitly* incorporated into a principle, it becomes a proposal of a different kind. As modified, it may escape my argument only because it is a different principle or because we are no longer to adhere to all of its implications.

I think many of us are dimly aware that the principles discussed here should be modified or overriden for the kinds of counterexamples I present. In this sense, my argument should not be surprising. It can be interpreted as a recommendation about the *spirit* in which we are to take these principles. It is meant to make explicit limitations and qualifications that should not be controversial. But these are limitations and qualifications that cannot go unstated; they must be made explicit. Hence I am not arguing that these principles must be rejected in their entirety. Rather, my claim is that they must be qualified or limited in certain specific ways. For only if they are modified in these ways will they be protected from some obvious objections.

This book is the result of a series of failures—failures on the part of the author to formulate defensible versions of the kinds of principles discussed here. I now believe that those failures can be explained by a general diagnosis—one that applies not only to my efforts but also to those of many others.

Principles with widely varying ideological implications are all subject to this argument. It applies, for example, to the libertarian theory of Robert Nozick, to the liberal theory of John Rawls, and to the socialist proposals of radical egalitarians. It also applies to democratic theories that prescribe majority rule, unanimity, or any other procedural principle. Similarly, it applies to utilitarianism in all its varieties, from the classical versions to their descendents in "cost-benefit" analysis and modern welfare economics. This critique applies to virtually every ethical criterion currently prominent in discussions of social choice. All of these criteria, if applied without exceptions or qualifications, would legitimate policies that impose severe deprivations when alternative policies that would impose no severe deprivations whatsoever were available.

Rather than apply this argument to a variegated list of individual principles, I apply it systematically to three broad categories of ethical criteria. All principles of these three kinds, if applied without exceptions or qualifications, would legitimate tyranny in the sense defined here.

The principles I discuss are all criteria for morally legitimate social choices. These choices may take place at either of two levels. Sometimes they will be *constitutional* choices, that is, choices among alternative forms of government. Sometimes they will be *policy* choices, that is, choices among alternatives available to the government within some ongoing constitutional order. Principles for morally legitimate social choices at either level are referred to, more briefly, as *legitimacy criteria.*[1]

My argument concerns three general kinds of legitimacy criteria:

1. Procedural principles, *such as majority rule, unanimity, and theories* *of consent. These are principles that prescribe adherence to a decision rule.*

2. Structural principles, *such as equality, utilitarianism, and Rawls's theory of justice. These are principles that prescribe a structure of distribution.*

3. Absolute rights principles, *such as the famous recent theory of Robert Nozick. These are principles that prescribe that a person must never experience consequences (or consequences brought about in certain ways) that would violate his rights.*

All of these principles would legitimate tyranny in the sense discussed here. Unless these principles are reformulated so as to permit exceptions or qualifications, they would all support government policies that would impose severe deprivations when alternative policies would impose no severe deprivations whatsoever. Before exploring these three general categories of principles, let us consider a case of tyranny from each category. Let us consider cases of tyranny applying to these three principles: majority rule (a procedural principle), equality (a structural principle), and Nozick's proposal (an absolute rights principle).

In August 1972, President Idi Amin ordered the expulsion, within ninety days, of approximately 50,000 Asians in Uganda. Those who considered staying were threatened with detention in military camps. There were strange disappearances, beatings, robberies, and apparent murders. Tens of thousands of Asians, who had built up a position of hard-won prosperity over several generations, were forced to leave the country virtually penniless. Many of those expelled were Ungandan citizens who became stateless persons after their papers were confiscated. Those who survived cruel treatment at the hands of the Ugandan authorities eventually found refuge in some fifteen countries—principally Great Britain.

An important fact about this episode is that Amin's treatment of the Asians was resoundingly popular among black Ugandans.[2] Let us imagine that before expelling the Asians, Amin had held a procedurally fair plebiscite on the issue. Could he then have justified the policy by invoking the principle of majority rule? Would we approve the policy merely because its popularity had been demonstrated?

It should be obvious that majorities—like all other governing coalitions—may commit acts of tyranny. And when they do, the principle of majority rule cannot be allowed to justify the results.

Another important fact about this episode is that the Ugandan government attempted to justify it as a measure that would redistribute the economy into the hands of black Africans. While it was not successful as a redistributive policy, let us imagine, hypothetically, our reaction to it *if* it had been. Suppose that redistributing the wealth of the Asians—their businesses, homes, and other assets—greatly increased equality in the distribution of income and wealth in Uganda. We might even consider such a policy of redistribution separate from the actual expulsion of the Asians. Suppose that instead of being expelled, they were forced, in a similarly brutal way, into the lowliest positions—or into the countryside (as Amin, at one point, threatened)—after their businesses, homes, and assets were redistributed to black Ugandans.

Would we approve such treatment of the Asians merely because it increased equality in the distribution of income and wealth? Surely we are compelled to ask: If more equality is desired, is there not some *other* way of attaining it? Some way that does not impose such severe deprivations on the Asian minority—or on anyone else? Some way that, while perhaps demanding sacrifices, does not impose such severe consequences on any particular group?

My objection to the principle of equality here is that even *if* there were such a nontyrannous route to greater equality, the principle of equality would be entirely insensitive to it. It would have us be *indifferent* between (a) the Ugandan strategy of equalization and (b) a nontyrannous route accomplishing the same end. For if these two policies lead to the same degree of equality, then on that principle, there is no moral issue in choosing (a) rather than (b). We *could not be wrong* in choosing the Ugandan strategy. The fact that one policy would impose such severe deprivations on the Asians counts for nothing in comparing them. As long as the final result is a more equal distribution, equality would legitimate this kind of tyranny.

Now let us imagine a quite different situation. Suppose that the Asians are not the richest, but rather, the poorest minority. And suppose further that there is a temporary food shortage that threatens the poorest sections of the country with starvation. And let us imagine that even though food has been stockpiled for just such an emergency, the government—perhaps in realizing that it is only the Asians who would be saved from starvation —does nothing.

Nozick's theory of absolute rights could be invoked by the government to legitimate such a policy of inaction. For Nozick's theory provides only one basis for evaluating a policy: Does it violate rights? And rights in Nozick's sense can be violated only when certain "side-constraints" are crossed—when actions of force, theft, or fraud interfere with someone's "entitlements" or cross someone's "boundaries." In this case, if the government chose inaction, no "side-constraints" would be violated. Everyone's "rights" would remain intact and everyone's "boundaries" would remain uncrossed if the government were to do nothing at all.[3]

The crucial fact about an absolute rights theory such as Nozick's is that moral prescriptions follow *only* from rights violations. It is this simplicity that provides such a theory, apparently, with much of its appeal. But it is also this simplicity that renders it indifferent between alternatives that *all* avoid violating rights. According to this kind of theory, all such alternatives must be equally good.

Compare two alternatives in this case: (a) the policy of saving the Asians from starvation, and (b) the policy of doing nothing. Neither of these policies violates rights in Nozick's sense. There would be no moral issue—in terms of the absolute rights theory—in choosing (b) rather than (a)—even though the Asians would starve, needlessly, if (b) were chosen. On Nozick's theory, we *could not be wrong* if we chose (b) rather than (a). One must be fully as good as the other. The starvation of the Asians—as long as it does not result from a rights violation—counts for nothing. It is such tyranny —through omission—that would be legitimated by Nozick's theory.

Majority rule, equality, and Nozick's theory would all legitimate tyrannous choices in these Ugandan examples. But this defect is not special to these three principles, and it is not special to variations on Uganda. The possibility of tyranny is not exotic, and the range of principles that legitimate tyranny is enormous.

It is not just majority rule, it is all procedural principles that have this defect. Secondly, it is not just equality, it is all structural principles that have this defect. Lastly, it is not just Nozick's theory, it is all absolute rights theories that have this defect. If applied without exceptions or qualifications, principles of these three kinds would legitimate policies imposing severe deprivations when alternative policies would impose no severe deprivations whatsoever.

What, precisely, are the principles that are subject to this argument? Let us examine each of these categories in turn.

Procedural principles. By a procedural principle I mean a principle that specifies a rule of decision but that specifies nothing about the content of those decisions—apart from possible requirements that the rule of decision be maintained in the future. By a *rule of decision* I mean a requirement that support from certain combinations or persons (that is, certain numbers, proportions, or particular groups of persons,[4] perhaps in some specified order) is necessary and sufficient to produce legitimate actions by the state.

This requirement may be a decision rule in the ordinary sense, for example, a criterion (such as unanimity or majority rule) that support from some stated proportion of members (100 percent, say, or 50 percent + 1) be required for winning coalitions. But it might also specify support from any other combination of individuals. It might, for example, specify that the King (or the Party Central Committee) decide, or that a person chosen by lot decide. It might also be quite complex; different procedures may be required for different kinds of decisions.

As long as a criterion leaves open the possibility that *anything* may be done—provided it has support from the persons or groups specified by the decision rule—it is procedural in the proposed sense. Criteria that would define legitimate social choices as those preserving consent or unanimity or majority rule or political equality (conjoined with a specific decision rule) offer examples of procedural criteria.[5] In chapter 8 I demonstrate that *every* principle of this kind has the defect that it would legitimate tyranny if it is adhered to without exceptions or qualifications.

Structural principles. Consider these principles: equality, maximin justice (the notion that the minimum share should be maximized, as advocated by John Rawls[6]), and utilitarianism (average utilitarianism, classical utilitarianism, and the criteria for cost-benefit analysis advocated by the "new welfare economics"). Consider also a powerful hybrid proposal by Douglas Rae combining utilitarianism with equality as follows: (1) When a choice is available that would make some stratum of society better off and no stratum of society worse off, select that; (2) When no such choice is available (serving the "general advantage" of society) choose the more *equal* alternative.[7]

What do all of these principles have in common? They share this property: they will judge any state of affairs X to be better, worse, or equal to any state of affairs Y, based merely on the information available from an account of payoffs to positions under X and under Y. By *payoffs* I mean goods[8] or welfare in a sense specified by the principle; by *positions* I mean either individuals listed in the order of their share of goods or welfare, or numerically equal groupings of individuals (n-tiles, each consisting of 1/nth of the population) listed in order of their shares of goods or welfare.

In other words, given a listing of payoffs to positions such as in table 1.1,

Table 1.1

X		Y	
Positions	*Payoffs*	*Positions*	*Payoffs*
P_1	X_1	P_1	Y_1
P_2	X_2	P_2	Y_2
P_3	X_3	P_3	Y_3
P_4	X_4	P_4	Y_4
P_5	X_5	P_5	Y_5

any *structural* principle will choose either X or Y or will rate them as precisely equal. It requires no other information than that available from such a table where X_1 is the payoff (in goods or welfare) to the first position under X and Y_1 is the payoff to the first position under Y, and so on. By comparing such payoffs to positions for situation X and situation Y, a structural principle will determine a choice.

It is important, in order for a principle to be structural in this sense, that the positions be identified anonymously in terms of a ranking of goods or welfare; it is not particular individuals whose payoffs are compared under X and Y but, rather, ranked positions. Structural principles say nothing, in other words, about how particular persons match up to positions under X as compared to how they match up under Y. As long as the structure of the situation (as judged by payoffs to positions) is improved, principles of this kind will support the choice of that structure—regardless of how persons are moved from one position to another in order to achieve that structure. This is a characteristic of these principles to which we shall return.

Some structural principles do not even require that the society be subdivided into numerically equal positions. They could just as well treat the entire society as a single "position" and choose between X and Y simply on the basis of the aggregate goods or welfare under X compared to the aggregate goods or welfare under Y. It is characteristic of the utilitarian family of principles that they require only such limited information. Of course, the additional information provided when positions are subdivided does not prevent them from determining choices. The total amounts of goods or welfare under X and Y can always be determined from a table such as table 1.1.

Equality is, of course, another important example of a structural principle. There are various measures of equality that would permit us to calculate whether X or Y was the more equal alternative in table 1.1 (provided that we knew the values of the payoffs to each position). We might, for example, choose whichever distribution minimized the differences of each position from the average payoff. Or we might adopt any one of several other measures of equality.[9]

Rawls's general conception of justice offers another structural principle in this sense. According to that conception we should maximize the minimum share of "primary goods."[10] If Rawlsian primary goods are interpreted as the payoffs, then Rawls's general conception would have us select the state of affairs with the highest minimum share. This "maximin" criterion obviously requires no information apart from that available from a table such as table 1.1. Furthermore, if Rawls's alternative formulation of justice (his "special conception") is compatible with the "maximin" notion of the "general conception," then it must also fall within the argument. For more on this issue, see chapters 12 and 13.

Reflection on the information offered by a table such as table 1.1 easily supports the conclusion that the range of principles that qualify as "structural" is enormous. I believe that most of the criteria commonly applied to the ethics of social choice are "structural" in this sense. In chapters 10 and 11 I demonstrate that all of these principles have the defect that they would legitimate tyranny if they were applied without exceptions or qualifications.

Absolute rights. The remaining group of principles posits absolute rights. An absolute rights principle is one that judges any social choice to be legitimate or illegitimate according to whether it conforms to the injunction: Never violate the rights of anyone. Following this injunction is taken to be necessary and sufficient for a legitimate social choice; violation of this injunction is taken to be sufficient for the illegitimacy of a social choice.

It is important to distinguish, as Nozick does, between rights theories that prohibit *any* action violating rights (these theories I will call absolute) and those that sometimes permit the violation of rights—but only in order to prevent some greater violations of rights. The latter kind of theory, in balancing one violation of rights against another, he calls a "utilitarianism of rights."[11]

Nozick's theory prescribes absolute rights and not a utilitarianism of rights in this sense. His theory would not, in other words, permit the state to violate *any* rights. It is all rights theories of this absolute kind that my argument is directed against in chapter 9.

All absolute rights principles, all structural principles, and all procedural principles share the fatal defects of principle X. If applied without exceptions or qualifications they would all legitimate policies imposing severe deprivations when alternative policies would impose no severe deprivations on anyone. They are all vulnerable to variations on our Ugandan theme: They would all legitimate tyranny.

2. The Problem of Tyranny

In his classic discussion of democratic theory, Robert Dahl confronts a problem that recurs "like a nagging tooth." It is "Madison's problem of majority tyranny."[1] In this section let us examine a portion of that problem: What acts by the government would be tyrannous whether they were supported by majorities or by coalitions of any other size?

American political thought, has, of course, long been preoccupied with this problem. According to Commager, one of its recurring themes has been "that governments are limited, that there are things no government may do, rights no government may impair, powers no government may exercise."[2] Yet defining these "things no government may do" is more troublesome than it may at first appear.

In Madison's time, however, there was something approaching an "American consensus"[3] that might be broadly sketched as follows: There are certain "inherent" or "inalienable rights"; the most fundamental aim of government is the preservation of those rights; any government that deprives men of those rights is an intolerable oppression or tyranny. Elements of this consensus can be seen in the most famous document of the period, the Declaration of Independence. It was the destruction of "unalienable rights" that justified a change of government. It is such rights, the Declaration declares, that define the very purpose of government: ". . . to secure these rights, Governments are instituted among Men. . . ." It is worth noting that Jefferson claimed no originality for these thoughts. Rather he wished "but to place before Mankind the common sense of the subject, in terms so plain and firm as to command their assent."[4]

In light of this consensus, Madison's operative definition of tyranny should not be surprising. In Dahl's careful reconstruction,[5] it is: "Tyranny is every severe deprivation of a natural right."[6]

The design of a nontyrannical constitutional system—one that would secure such natural rights—was the problem that engaged Madison and the founding fathers. But their awareness that a majoritarian system might place the rights of minorities at risk complicated that task enormously. As Madison argued in the *Federalist*, "It is of great importance in a republic not only to guard the society against the oppression of its rulers, but to guard one part of the society against the injustice of the other part. Different interests necessarily exist in different classes of citizens. If a majority be united by a common interest, the rights of the minority will be insecure."[7]

As Dahl summarizes the problem of constitutional choice that faced Madison: "Is it possible to construct a system for arriving at decisions that is compatible with the idea of political equality and at the same time protects the rights of minorities?"[8] Is it possible to design a system compatible with the "republican principle" of majority rule[9] on the one hand, and the rights of minorities on the other? Is it possible, in other words, to institute the fundamental "goal" of the Madisonian system—a "non-tyrannical republic"?[10]

This question can only be pursued if a conception of "tyranny" is more adequately specified. It will immediately be seen that although Madison's operative definition of "tyranny" is suggestive, it is clearly inadequate as it stands. In the rest of this chapter I critically examine both this Madisonian definition of tyranny and a modern definition that Dahl proposes as an "analogue" to it. In chapter 3 I propose an alternative definition that, I believe, avoids difficulties in both of these formulations.

The most obvious difficulty facing any modern application of Madison's definition is the elusiveness of a rigorous and convincing formulation of natural rights. However, even if we were to assume some precise specification of rights roughly analogous to the "natural rights" commonly invoked in public debates in Madison's time, we would face another formidable difficulty. Since, "at a minimum, *any* curtailment of natural rights without one's 'consent' was a sufficiently severe deprivation to constitute tyranny,"[11] and since natural rights may conflict irreconcilably in particular cases, there are cases where no matter what the government does, it has deprived *someone* of his rights. A's right to life, for example, may conflict with B's right to liberty, or B's right to liberty may conflict with C's right to property. There are situations where someone's rights will be deprived by any possible action or inaction of the government. All of the formulations of natural rights which were current in Madison's time are clearly subject to this possibility.[12]

In such a situation,[13] Madison's definition would lead to our classifying the government as a "tyranny" no matter what it chooses. For no matter what the government does in such a case, it will deprive someone of rights. Furthermore, if we assume (as I do throughout this essay) that one characteristic of "tyrannous" actions is that they are ethically wrong, then such a situation would define a moral "blind alley"[14]—a case where *every* alternative is wrong. Because the definition of tyranny is formulated in strong terms—without *ceteris paribus* clauses or provisions for balancing one violation of rights against another—*every* alternative would be absolutely proscribed. The advocate of such a criterion finds himself in an untenable —indeed, in a logically inconsistent—position if his principle produces such conflicting injunctions.[15]

This is, of course, only one of the difficulties with Madison's formulation. Dahl's critique cogently focuses on the ambiguities in the notion of "natural rights" and on the difficulties of any procedural formula by which those rights might be better specified.[16]

Dahl's response to these difficulties is a bold proposal of his own—an argument "essentially ethical in character," for considering "intensities" of preference in a definition of tyranny.[17] This notion of accounting for *intensities* as well as numbers (at least in our ethical judgments, if not in our institutional mechanisms) is highlighted in the distinction between what Dahl calls the "severe symmetrical disagreement" of figure 2.1 and the "severe asymmetrical disagreement" of figure 2.2.[18] In the symmetrical case, an intense minority faces an equally intense majority, while in the asymmetrical case the intensity of the minority is balanced only by apathy in the majority. In this latter case the overall balance of opinion would rest with the minority. It is this asymmetrical case that, Dahl implies, is most objectionable. For an apathetic majority to overrule a sufficiently intense minority would by "tyranny": "If there is any case that might be considered the modern analogue to Madison's implicit concept of tyranny, I suppose it is this one."[19] While I will argue that this distinction between the symmetrical and asymmetrical cases is *not* adequate for the definition of tyranny, I will at a later point incorporate certain aspects of Dahl's proposal into my own definition.

For the moment, however, let us examine Dahl's proposal. I will argue that the distinction between asymmetrical and symmetrical cases does not usefully distinguish tyrannous from nontyrannous cases. It leads to the

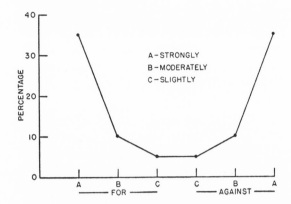

Figure 2.1. Severe disagreement: symmetrical. Source: Robert Dahl, *A Preface to Democratic Theory* (Chicago: University of Chicago Press, 1956). Reprinted with permission of the publisher.

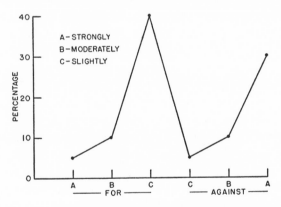

Figure 2.2. Severe disagreement: asymmetrical. Source: Robert Dahl, *A Preface to Democratic Theory* (Chicago: University of Chicago Press, 1956). Reprinted with permission of the publisher.

misclassification of some tyrannous cases as nontyrannous, and of some nontyrannous cases as tyrannous. I will offer, in other words, asymmetrical cases of nontyranny and symmetrical cases of tyranny.

First, let us begin with a central and obvious case of tyranny (in the general Madisonian sense summarized by Dahl as "severe deprivation of a natural right"). Let us imagine a minority group (say Jews in a state like Nazi Germany) whose extermination is voted by majority rule in a pro-

cedurally fair election (my example has been made intentionally hypothetical). Let us imagine, to begin with, that only a few of the majority feel
strongly about this issue (the rest being quite apathetic), but that all of the
minority, of course, feel extraordinary intensity about the issue. This would
appear to offer the classic example of severe asymmetrical disagreement as
a model for tyranny as pictured in figure 2.2. The intensity of the minority
may outweigh the numbers of the majority so as to make it tyrannous to
overrule the former.

Suppose, however, that the example is altered slightly. Suppose that the
majority is not so apathetic. Suppose that the issue and the distribution of
preferences are precisely as before except that the Nazis in the majority are
simply *more enthusiastic*. I submit that whatever ethical reasons we have
for classifying as tyrannous the acts upon the minority in the first example,
we could apply them as well to the second example. The majority extermination of the minority would seem tyrannous in *either* case: The distinction
between the severe asymmetrical and the severe symmetrical cases does
not properly mark the dividing line.

Consider now another (less dramatic) example. Suppose there is an
ongoing policy of Prohibition. Suppose, further, that there is a minority of
extremely zealous supporters of the policy and that, over time, there also
develops a largely apathetic majority that favors repeal. Would it be
tyrannous for the less intense majority to overrule such a minority? The
members of the minority feel intensely about whether *others* should be
permitted to drink (*they* will, of course, continue to abstain). I believe that
if the issues are this simple, it could not be tyrannous to overrule such a
minority. One way of explaining this conclusion is to return to the fundamental (but vague) Madisonian view cited by Dahl: There is no way in
which *that* minority could claim "a severe deprivation of *its* natural rights."
It is its preferences concerning the behavior of *others* that is at issue.

If I am right in these inferences, the Prohibition case is asymmetrical
nontyranny and the Nazi case (as modified) is symmetrical tyranny. But
then does "intensity" have anything to do with tyranny? I will take the
position here that it does. There are certain kinds of intense preferences
that define severe deprivations. And it is tyrannous, I believe, for a
government to impose severe deprivations when an alternative policy would
impose no severe deprivations on anyone.

But before this claim can be developed into a workable definition, a
more extensive discussion of severe deprivations and intensity is required.

This is my concern in the following chapters. My aim is a definition of tyranny that both avoids the blind-alley problem of the original Madisonian formula and also properly classifies the Nazi and Prohibition cases just discussed—treating the former, but not the latter, as an instance of tyranny.

3. The Dilemma of Real Interests

I have just referred to the "tyranny" of a government imposing severe deprivations when such deprivations were entirely avoidable. This notion can be defined more precisely as follows:

1. *A policy choice by the government is an instance of simple tyranny when that policy imposes severe deprivations even though an alternative policy would have imposed no severe deprivations on anyone.*

I use the term "simple tyranny" because I mean to select from all of the varied and contested usages of the word *tyranny* certain cases that are both compelling and straightforward. I believe these cases are straightforward because the severe deprivations that result from simple tyranny are deprivations that could have been *entirely* avoided for everyone. These cases avoid the complexities of tragic choices where *someone* must suffer severely no matter which policy is chosen. I do not wish to deny that some cases of this latter kind might also justifiably be termed "tyrannous." However, these tragic choices lack the simplicity of tyranny in the sense defined here. In the argument that follows I mean by the term "tyranny" what I have just defined as "simple tyranny." There will be no need for us to deal with the possibility of more "complex" cases—although nothing I say here should be interpreted as ruling them out.

Many elements of this definition require further discussion. Even portions of it that appear relatively straightforward—such as the notion of severe deprivations being "imposed" and the notion of policies being "alternatives" to one another—require more elaboration.[1]

It may seem, as I explore each part of this definition, that I am belaboring the obvious. In fact, my argument would be strengthened if this definition, as fully developed, were so obvious as to be noncontroversial. For it is meant to define a class of counterexamples that will be systematically directed at other principles. If the reader can agree that tyranny, in this "simple" sense, must be avoided, he will have granted me the basis for my argument.

The crucial definition in this notion of "tyranny" is that of "severe deprivations." Exploring this notion requires several chapters. Let me begin by introducing another definition—which at this stage highlights our problem but does not resolve it:

2. *A severe deprivation is the destruction of an essential interest.*

It is when X's essential interests are destroyed even though an alternative policy would not have had comparable effects on anyone that severe deprivations take on the gratuitous and unjustified character of simple tyranny.

Note that this definition of tyranny would not require that a government *always* refrain from imposing severe deprivations. If we assume that a government is morally required to always avoid tyranny we are not thereby committed to the position that a government is morally required to always avoid imposing severe deprivations. For there will be cases where *every* alternative policy imposes severe deprivations on someone. In such cases, the definition of tyranny says nothing about what should be done. However, when there *is* a policy alternative that would not impose such severe deprivations on anyone, then the avoidance of tyranny offers a clear pre-scription.

Now it might be objected that this radical incompleteness is a fatal defect in the definition of tyranny. If it were meant as an all-purpose guide to policy choice, this objection would have merit. But I have proposed it with a more limited aim. This definition of simple tyranny is a way of singling out certain horrendous wrongs that any acceptable principle must avoid legitimating. It is not even meant to capture every possible wrong a government may commit, but only certain horrendous ones.

The argument is that if a principle were to legitimate wrongs of that kind, then it must be morally unacceptable. The interest of the argument is that virtually every ethical criterion for social choice currently under serious discussion would legitimate tyrannous choices of that kind. If applied without exceptions or qualifications, they would all legitimate severe deprivations when an alternative policy would not impose such deprivations on anyone.

In order to develop this argument we need an adequate definition of severe deprivations. We need an account of when a person's "essential interests" are destroyed. However, there are some fundamental difficulties facing any such effort to account for a person's interests. While not insurmountable, these difficulties are sufficiently important to be acknowledged at the outset.

Any theory of interests faces a twofold difficulty. On the one hand, a theory may define a person X's interests in terms of the satisfaction of X's *actual* wants or preferences. Such a theory faces the problem of interpersonal comparisons of intensity. On the other hand, a theory may define X's interests in a way that diverges from *all* of X's actual wants or preferences. Such a theory faces the problem of justifying paternalistic judgments, that is, judgments about the interests of X that may differ from all of X's own notions about his interests.[2]

More precisely, a principle is vulnerable to the problem of interpersonal comparisons if it adheres to *citizen sovereignty*. A principle adheres to citizen sovereignty if it judges a person X to be better off if, and only if, some of X's actual preferences are satisfied. The citizen is sovereign in the sense that it is *his* wants that must be satisfied if we are to say he is better off.

I will adapt some terminology from Brian Barry (which he employs for a different purpose) by saying that principles with an account of interests that conform to citizen sovereignty are *want-regarding* because they define X's interests in terms of the satisfaction of at least some of his *actual* wants. On the other hand, principles that depart from citizen sovereignty are *ideal-regarding* because they define X's interests in a way that may depart from all of X's actual wants.[3] Hence it is want-regarding accounts of interests that face the problem of the interpersonal comparison of intensities, while it is ideal-regarding accounts of interests that face the problem of paternalistic judgments. These two possibilities combine to pose a dilemma I call the "dilemma of real interests."

But what is the difficulty with interpersonal comparisons of the intensity of preferences? The classic statement of the problem comes from Lord Robbins. In an influential article written in 1938 he described how he came to abandon a utilitarian ("Benthamite") position by citing this illustration: ". . . the story of how an Indian official had attempted to explain to a high-caste Brahmin the sanctions of the Benthamite system. "'But that,'" said the Brahmin, "'cannot possibly be right. I am ten times as capable of happiness as that untouchable over there.'"[4]

While Robbins did not sympathize with the Brahmin, he had to confess: "I could not escape the conviction that, if I chose to regard men as equally capable of satisfaction and he to regard them as differing according to a hierarchical schedule, the difference between us was not one which could be resolved by the same methods of demonstration as were available in other fields of social judgment."[5]

The difficulty Robbins saw in interpersonal comparisons was clearest in a remark of Jevons, which he quoted approvingly: "I see no means whereby such comparison can be accomplished. *Every mind is inscrutable to every other mind and no common denominator of feeling is possible.*"[6]

If minds are "inscrutable" in this way, then it would be impossible to compare the extent to which A prefers one alternative to another with the extent to which B prefers one alternative to another. The comparative strength of the preferences of A and B is the issue (or, expressed another way, the issue is the magnitude of the utilities they would each experience if those preferences were satisfied).[7]

Now if such a claim about the inscrutability of other minds is taken seriously, then the range of judgments available to want-regarding principles appears extremely limited. Notice that *some* judgments are still possible because the postulate is not meant to rule out *intra*personal comparisons — Robbins speaks explicitly of "introspection" as one form of evidence that would, in fact, be available.[8]

Imagine a series of wells. Suppose we had some means of telling whether each well increased or decreased in its store of water—but we had no information about how an increase or decrease in one well compared to an increase or decrease in another. We could determine the direction of any changes, but not the amount. Even within these limitations, if we knew that the water level in at least one well had increased, and that the level in no well had decreased, we could conclude that the aggregate amount of water in the wells must have increased.[9]

Apply analogous limitations to a group of individuals: each individual can tell us whether his satisfaction has increased or decreased—but we have no information about how an increase or decrease in one individual compares to that of another. If we knew that at least one individual's level of satisfaction had increased and that no individual's level of satisfaction had decreased, we could conclude that aggregate satisfaction among these individuals must have increased. We could reach this conclusion without the necessity of any *inter*personal comparisons whatsoever. The only judgments required are *intra*personal ones.

In this way a utilitarian who became skeptical, as Lord Robbins did, about the possibility of any interpersonal comparisons, would find himself committed, nevertheless, to every judgment sanctioned by the Pareto principle. For the Pareto principle is the principle that if a change would increase the level of satisfaction of at least one individual, and if it would decrease the level of no one, then it must be approved.

The limited range of judgments that this strategy permits can be seen in the simple two-person case illustrated in figure 3.1. Suppose U_A is the

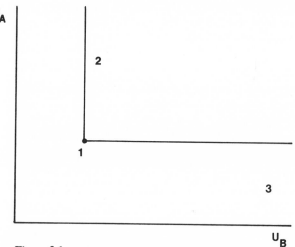

Figure 3.1.

utility to person A and suppose U_B is the utility to person B. The visual representation of U_A and U_B might be imagined to be made of elastic: they are ordinal scales. Just as in the water-wells analogy, there is no comparative basis for judgments of magnitude. While the *ordering* of points along U_A and U_B tells us whether their satisfaction has increased or decreased, we know nothing about how increases or decreases along U_A compare to increases or decreases along U_B.

Suppose our status quo is point 1. The Pareto principle tells us that any point in the quadrant *northeast* of 1 is to be preferred. For any such point (for example, point 2) will make at least one person better off and no one worse off than at point 1.

However, if the question arose whether we should move from point 1 to point 3, the Pareto principle would offer us no basis whatsoever for a response. For unless one point is within a quadrant northeast of another, the Pareto principle tells us nothing at all about how to compare them.

It is as if, in the water-wells analogy, someone had asked us if the aggregate level of water had increased after some wells had gone down and others had gone up. Having information about the *direction* of change in each well, but no information about the *magnitude* of those changes, we would have no basis for a response. Given these limitations on our knowledge, the new aggregate level would remain a complete mystery.

Unless one point falls within a quadrant northeast of another, the Pareto principle says nothing about how the two points are to be compared. But this means we will be extremely limited in the choices we can evaluate. As Little, discussing these Paretian limitations, concludes, "No change of any significance in the real world could ever be made without harming some people."[10] Once even one person is harmed—while others are benefited —the Pareto principle is silenced.

But while silence on most social issues would be the result of sticking to the Paretian limitations, the problem of interpersonal comparisons arises immediately if one ventures beyond those limits. For any such principle would be committed to choices that make some people better off and some worse off. Are these choices to be justified without an account of how the benefits to some compare to the harms to others? How can a principle justify imposing harms and benefits unless it accounts, in some way, for how they compare to one another? The difficulty is that any such account must respond to the alleged "inscrutability" of one mind to another.

A critique of one famous set of responses to this problem is offered in chapter 11. My own more limited response is presented in the chapters immediately following this one.

But this problem of interpersonal comparisons of intensity arises for want-regarding principles. If a principle offers an account of interests that requires no assessment of the satisfaction of any *actual* wants, preferences, or desires, it may avoid this problem entirely. However, principles of this *ideal*-regarding kind face a fundamental difficulty of a different sort.

The defining characteristic of ideal-regarding principles is that their account of interests does not conform to citizen sovereignty: a claim that

X's interests are served does not require a claim that (at least some of) his actual wants, aims, or preferences are satisfied. Some other account of X's interests, an ideal-regarding account, is offered instead.

Such an ideal-regarding theory must justify paternalistic inferences: that X's interests are served by some change even though none of X's own actual wants, aims, or preferences are satisfied by that change. In such cases, ideal-regarding theories would interpret X's interests quite differently from the way in which X himself interprets them.[11]

Consider a central case: Rawlsian "primary goods." An agent in the "original position" is to select principles of justice in his rational self-interest under fair conditions for considering that self-interest. He is to select a moral principle without knowing his own position in the society—or any other information that might allow him to bias the choice of principles in his own favor. In this thought experiment, one kind of information denied to him is any knowledge of his own *actual* aims, wants, or preferences. An agent knows only a "thin theory" of his "good," that is, of his interests; he knows only information about his own good that applies equally to everyone else. Rawls posits a rational preference for certain "primary goods" as the account of self-interest an agent can use for choosing principles of justice.[12]

An agent is assumed to have such a rational preference for primary goods because primary goods would further what is called his "rational plan of life." Note, however, that an agent's rational plan of life is not necessarily something of which he is conscious—even in actual life. It is the plan that *would* be chosen with "full deliberative rationality."[13] If an agent *could* rationally choose his plan of life "with full awareness of the relevant facts and after a careful consideration of the consequences,"[14] then this is the plan he would choose. "A rational plan," we are told, "is one that *would* be selected if certain conditions were fulfilled."[15] Primary goods are preferred, in the original position, because they would further such a hypothetically rational plan.

This theory is clearly ideal-regarding[16] in that an agent in the original position is held to interpret his share of primary goods as an account of his own self-interest. Whether or not he prefers more of such goods to less in actual life, in the original position, his interests are defined in that way. Furthermore, he is held to prefer those primary goods in a certain order. Regardless of his actual plan of life, his interests are said to be furthered by a society organized so as to provide these primary goods to everyone in this lexical (or absolutely rigid) order: first liberty, then fair equal opportunity, then income and wealth.

This theory of self-interest is a hypothetically rational one. "The criterion of the good," we are told, "is *hypothetical* in a way similar to the criterion of justice."[17]

A central problem for Rawls's theory is the justification of this paternalistic inference:[18] X's interests are said to be furthered by increased shares of primary goods, in a given order, regardless of whether X himself believes that he is better off with such increased shares. It may be the case that *none* of X's own wants, preferences, aims, or desires require such increases; X is said to be better off, nevertheless. No knowledge of X's actual preferences in the matter are required for this inference that, rationally, X must be better off with more primary goods, allotted according to the hypothesized priority rankings.[19]

I believe Rawls's justification for this paternalistic inference to be deeply problematical.[20] However, there is no need to evaluate that account here. For my point is merely that Rawls's theory of primary goods, as an ideal-regarding theory, must provide such a justification. In offering such an ideal-regarding theory, Rawls must justify the inference that X must be better off, even if that inference conflicts with *all* of X's own wants, aims, or preferences.

The need for such a justification defines the second horn of a dilemma. This dilemma might be called the "dilemma of real interests." Do X's real interests consist in the satisfaction of (at least some of) his own actual wants, preferences, or aims? If so, then the principle is want-regarding and must respond to the problem of interpersonal comparisons.

Or, do X's real interests consist in something other than the satisfaction of (at least some of) his own actual wants, preferences, or aims? If so, then the principle is ideal-regarding and must justify such paternalistic inferences.

To the extent that a principle includes a want-regarding account of interests, it must respond to the first horn. To the extent that a principle includes an ideal-regarding account of interests, it must respond to the second. In the next chapters I offer an account of "essential interests" that includes *both* want-regarding and ideal-regarding elements. Hence in arguing for this account, I must respond to both problems. The adequacy of all that follows must be assessed against these two difficulties.

4. Life Plans and Essential Interests

As we have just seen, assessing interests is a murky business. Probably no single theory should presume to adequately define every person's interests in every situation. The definitions proposed here, however, have a more limited aim. They are not intended to define every interest of a person, but only his essential interests. It is the destruction of such essential interests—when an alternative policy would not have comparable effects—that constitutes simple tyranny.

In order to define *essential interests,* I will return to Dahl's "intensity" proposal. My position is that certain special kinds of intense preferences define essential interests.

First of all, it should be clear that not all intense preferences can be taken to define essential interests. In the Nazi case alluded to earlier, the Jews obviously would have essential interests at stake. But in the Prohibition case, however intense the sentiments of those who wish to enforce Prohibition, their essential interests do not appear to be at stake, for those intense preferences concern the behavior of others.

What we require, first of all, are classifications, not only for the intensity of preferences about a policy, but also for the kinds of consequences that may result from it. In another context, Barry distinguishes between wants that are "privately oriented" and those that are "publicly oriented." While he does not define these systematically, the distinction in its rough form can be put to use here:

By "privately-oriented" I mean having oneself (or at most one's family) as the reference group; or, more precisely, affecting oneself or one's family. When I speak of "being affected" here I mean having one's life materially impinged upon by some change in opportunities or routine. I do not mean being made to feel, as in the phrase "an affecting sight." Thus, in the sense of "being affected" relevant here a Swiss hotelkeeper, asked if he was affected by the war might reply that it decreased his trade but he could not reply that he was upset by the thought of cities being bombed. Or again, a Northern Negro in the U.S.A. is affected by discrimination which prevents him from getting certain jobs or houses, etc.; but he is not affected by what happens in the South.[1]

A similar distinction can be seen in the debate over "interdependence effects." Should a person's "resentment or envy of the achievements of others" be included in his utility? Is each person's utility in part a function of the real incomes of others, or are utilities not "interdependent" but "independent" ("the utility of each person depending on his own goods only")?[2] Such independent utilities would be restricted to privately oriented wants in Barry's sense, while interdependent utilities would include publicly oriented wants in Barry's sense.

While there are important questions about the precise dividing line between private- and public-regarding wants, a serviceable version of the distinction can be briefly sketched here. First of all, the distinction concerns *wants*. The wants classified here concern either *states of affairs* or *actions*. Turning to states of affairs, X's want for a given state of affairs is *public-regarding* to the extent that X wants some condition of *others* in that state of affairs. X's want for a given state of affairs is *private-regarding* to the extent that X wants some condition for *himself* that he does not conceive in terms of the condition of anyone else.

Hence, X's want for Y's happiness (or unhappiness) is public-regarding; X's want for X's own happiness is private-regarding. Even X's want to be made happy by Y's happiness or unhappiness (because X is altruistic or malevolent) must be public-regarding: It is a want of X to experience a given condition (to be made happy) that he conceives in terms of the condition of someone else (Y's happiness or unhappiness).[3]

Turning to actions, X's want that a given action be performed is private-regarding if it concerns *his* performances of the action; it is public-regarding if it concerns someone else's performance of the action. Similarly, X's want for his action to bring about a given state of affairs is *private*-regarding if it is a condition for *himself* in that state of affairs that he wants. X's want for his action to bring about a given state of affairs is *public*-regarding if it is a condition for *others* in that state of affairs that he wants.

Hence, the general point is that X's private-regarding wants concern his *own* actions and his own condition in any given state of affairs; alternatively, X's public-regarding wants concern the actions of *others* and the conditions of others in any given state of affairs.

Of course, private- and public-regarding wants are commonly intermixed. However, sorting them out is essential if the issues involved are to be clarified.

I grant that this may sometimes be difficult in practice. Some wants may not come attached to clear linguistic descriptions that can be classified in this way. In some cases the person himself may not know quite what he wants or why he wants it. This simply means that there will be problems of application to cases in which it is ambiguous what kinds of claims and interests are at stake.

If severe deprivations are defined in terms of wants that are *both* private-regarding and intense, then it could not be "tyranny" for the Prohibition advocates to be overruled. For not matter how intense their preferences, they are public-regarding—they are preferences about whether *others* should be permitted to drink. On the other hand, the Nazi case offers an obvious case of tyranny. For the preferences of those who would suffer from their policies are clearly *both* intense and private-regarding, while the Nazi preferences—no matter how intense—are clearly public-regarding. They are preferences that certain dreadful consequences be imposed on another group. According to our proposed definition of tyranny, if one policy imposes severe deprivations when an alternative would not, then choice of the former must be tyrannous.

However, we have said little, thus far, about what might be meant by *intensity*. In claiming that a person X feels "intensely" I do *not* mean that X's emotions have been aroused to a fever pitch (although that might also be the case), nor do I mean that X is experiencing extreme "sensate intensity" (although that might also be the case).[4] Rather, I mean that the issue is of crucial *importance* to him compared to any of his other private-regarding wants; by this I mean that it is of crucial importance within the framework of what might be called his "plan of life."

In order to clarify this notion of the crucial importance of certain private-regarding preferences, I will modify the Rawlsian notion that a person's interests are defined by his plan of life.[5] The basic notion is "that a person may be regarded as a human life lived according to a plan"[6] and that he can be defined as happy when he is in the process of successfully executing his plan.[7] But rather than defining the interests of a person with respect to a *hypothetical* plan, they are defined here with respect to a person's *actually adopted* plan—provided it is chosen with at least a minimal degree of autonomy.

All of these notions require further explanation. Let us begin with the notion of a "plan of life." The notion of a life plan does not require that people be preoccupied with planning ahead.[8] Not having an articulate or coherent plan can be regarded as the choice of a kind of plan. A plan of life is merely the structure of commitments, adopted over the course of a life, to various "projects,"[9] that is, wants and courses of action intended to fulfill those wants. These wants may, of course, be either public- or private-regarding. A course of action may be short- or long-term, and its connection to one's wants may be quite explicit or it may be only vaguely formulated. Since various commitments may be adopted separately, a person may never juxtapose them all together; he may never entertain the question of whether they cohere or whether he has been acting at cross-purposes. Nevertheless, it is these projects to which he is committed that give his life structure and meaning. Provided they have not been destroyed by certain kinds of coercive conditions, a person's projects may be taken as defining his interests—for they define his life.

We need not say much more about the general notion of a life plan, for it is only one particular portion of anyone's life plan that will concern us:

3. X's *personal life plan is the constellation of private-regarding wants and courses of action*[10] *to which he is committed.*

While an overall life plan has both private- and public-regarding elements, at its core must be a structure of private-regarding wants. This does not mean that the personal part of a life plan is necessarily the most important part. A person may be so devoted to altruistic causes that it is his public-regarding wants that are most important to him. Nevertheless, since it is *his* plan, he must figure in it somewhere. It must be a plan that applies to him. There must be some personal conditions that have value for him—even if they are only valued because they are necessary conditions for the achievement of his public-regarding aims.

X's personal life plan defines X's essential interests. Hence, to return to our problem of defining severe deprivations:

4. *A severe deprivation to X is the decisive defeat of X's personal life plan.*

Such a personal life plan can be decisively defeated in two ways:

5. *X's personal life plan has been decisively defeated*

a. *if it is prevented from ever developing with even a minimal degree of autonomy, or*

b. *if portions of it encounter reversals so important to X that X could not be fully compensated by the fulfillment of any of his other private-regarding wants.* [11]

Both the (a) and (b) portions of this definition require some explanation. The (a) portion defines our topic in the next chapter: If certain basic human requirements are not satisfied, X will not be able to develop his life plan with even a minimal degree of autonomy—for coercive conditions, perhaps threatening his very survival, will distort all of his aspirations. Let us set the (a) portion of the definition aside, for this topic requires a separate chapter.

Turning to the (b) portion, I take the notion of "compensation" from economics: X is compensated for an event that makes him worse off if he would be *indifferent* between two situations (or prefer the latter to the former): (1) his situation *before* the event and *without* the compensation, and (2) his situation *after* the event and *with* the compensation. He must be fully satisfied with the compensation *in his own estimation.* This can be expressed in more technical terms by saying that he must be on at least as high an indifference curve after the compensation as he was before the event for which he is being compensated.

To say that there are *no* other private-regarding preferences that, if satisfied, would compensate a person for a reversal (evaluated in terms of a private-regarding preference) is to attribute extraordinary centrality to that preference. It must be of paramount importance to him.

Perhaps his physical safety is at stake; or perhaps it is his entire life's work. Or perhaps such fundamental moral or religious convictions are at stake that were X to be forced to sacrifice them, he would no longer regard life as worth continuing. [12] In such cases, it is plausible to imagine that no other private-regarding preferences, if fulfilled, could fully compensate X for such a reversal.

Note that this notion of compensation does not require money to be the compensating variable. While X could be compensated with money, he could also be compensated with anything else he values—with the fulfill-ment of *any* of his other private-regarding aspirations. Only if his reversal were so severe that *none* of these could compensate him could we say that his personal life plan has been decisively defeated. It is decisively defeated only if his reversal is so severe that it could not be rendered commensurable with benefits rendered in terms of any of the other things he values.

Unlike some uses of the compensation argument, this formulation avoids bias resulting from the existing distribution of income.[13] For money is only one among innumerable forms of compensation. Only if X's setback is so severe that he cannot be fully compensated (he cannot regard himself as equally well off with the setback *and* the compensation as he was without them both) has he suffered a severe deprivation.

Another interesting property of this definition is that it requires no interpersonal comparisons of the intensity of preference.[14] The only judgments of intensity are *intra*personal: X suffers a severe deprivation if his reversal, in terms of a given private-regarding preference, is so extreme that being made better off in terms of any of his other private-regarding preferences cannot fully compensate him in his own estimation. The question of how his preferences compare, in some sense, to someone else's never arises.

There is, of course, an interpersonal comparison here—but it is not one that concerns the comparative intensity of preferences. It is the explicit value judgment that each person's most essential interests (that is, those most essential to him in the sense specified) are comparable in importance to any other person's most essential interests. In this sense an *interpersonal comparison of interests* has been accomplished without an interpersonal comparison of the intensity of preference taking place.

In any consideration of alternative policies, each person may be regarded as having (to borrow a suggestive analogy of Ronald Dworkin) a "trump." Dworkin argues that "rights trump goals." While his proposal is quite different,[15] our proposal might be summarized as "severe deprivations trump other moral claims." If X will suffer a severe deprivation, and no one else has a similar interest at stake, then regardless of whatever other claims are involved, X carries the day. However, if every alternative involves severe deprivations for someone, then the results are undecidable within this framework. For the only claim being made is that "severe deprivations trump (that is, outrank or override) other moral claims."

In applying the definition of tyranny we regard each person as entitled to those "trumps" defined by his personal life plan. The identification of cases of tyranny requires no interpersonal comparison of the relative claim of those "trumps." For the tyrannous cases are precisely those where a policy is chosen that destroys essential interests (that is, imposes severe deprivations) when an alternative policy would *not* have done that to anyone. In such a case, if such a nondeprivating alternative is not chosen, the result is tyranny. No comparison of the "severity" of the severe deprivations is ever required to identify a case of tyranny.

Of course, a complete theory would tell us how to compare severe deprivations and also how to choose among nondeprivating alternatives. But such a complete theory would face more extreme cases of the two difficulties sketched in the last chapter—the interpersonal comparison of intensities (for its want-regarding elements) and the problem of paternalistic judgments (for its ideal-regarding elements).

If I am correct in believing that the interpersonal-comparison-of-intensities problem has been avoided, it is only because I have chosen a strategy of incompleteness roughly analogous to that of the Pareto principle. If, despite this incompleteness, the principle serves to identify certain horrendous choices that any adequate principle must avoid, then my strategy will have succeeded thus far.

However, there are ideal-regarding elements to the definition, as well. Such elements must face the corresponding challenge of justifying paternalistic judgments. I examine how well this portion of the proposal fares in the next chapter.

5. Subsistence Needs and Life Chances

In the last chapter I argued that the decisive defeat of an individual's personal life plan should be considered a severe deprivation. But there were two general ways, I claimed, in which such a life plan can be decisively defeated. First, while in progress, it may suffer an extreme reversal. Defeats of this kind were discussed in the last chapter. Second, there may be conditions that prevent it from ever developing—or at least from ever developing with what I called "even a minimal degree of autonomy." Defeats of this latter kind define my present topic.

But what do I mean by "even a minimal degree of autonomy"? I believe that a reasonable definition can be arrived at as follows: An individual is prevented from developing his personal life plan with even a minimal degree of autonomy if his choices are structured *coercively*. An individual's choices are structured coercively if either or both of these conditions obtain:

i. *Every available alternative offers a serious risk of disaster.*
ii. *No available alternative offers him prospects of success.*

This definition obviously requires that we offer interpretations of *disaster* and *success*. This task is complicated by the fact that we cannot do this explicitly in terms of the individual's preferences, for we are attempting to formulate the conditions within which those actual preferences must be permitted to develop. The idea is that unless certain conditions obtain, the individual's actual plan of life should not be taken as offering a reliable guide to his interests. Once these conditions do obtain, we can define severe deprivations in the terms offered in the last chapter. But if they do not obtain, we may claim severe deprivations even when the person involved is partially or completely unaware of the difficulty. In other words, we have now reached the ideal-regarding (rather than the want-regarding) step in the argument.

By specifying notions of *disaster* and *success* in (i) and (ii) above I will derive two conditions that must both obtain if X's life plan is to be permitted to develop with even a minimal degree of autonomy. From (i) I will derive a condition that X's choices permit security for his *subsistence needs;* from (ii) I will derive the condition that X have an *adequate life chance.*

It will soon be apparent that these conditions are not very demanding. Because the account of interests here is ideal-regarding, I have intentionally formulated only modest and fairly noncontroversial requirements. Nevertheless, if both of them are fulfilled for X, he could reasonably be said to develop his personal life plan under conditions that would permit (at least) a minimal degree of autonomy. It will soon be apparent that denial of either of these conditions produces deprivations at least as terrible as any of those discussed in the last chapter.

By *disaster* in (i) above, I mean the denial of subsistence needs. For if every alternative available to X offers a serious risk that his subsistence needs will be denied, then surely his choices have been structured in a coercive way. When subsistence is precarious, life proceeds within what might be called a "danger zone"[1]—a continuing threat that the most basic needs will not be met. Everything must then be bent to the purpose of ensuring survival. Decisions that would otherwise appear patently irrational become explicable by the effort to provide securely for subsistence needs.

James Scott has documented this phenomenon in various peasant economies. For example, peasants will put up with an exploitative[2] tenancy system rather than perform wage labor for higher average returns, because as tenants provision for their subsistence needs is more secure. Similarly, peasants will resist innovations, such as alternative crops, which offer much higher average returns, because they would also increase the risk of falling below subsistence. Within the "danger zone" every choice is distorted by the coercive influence of the threat to subsistence.

Sometimes the cumulative impact of such coercion distorts preferences to the point where people come to accept—or even to welcome—further miseries. They reach a point where additional privations are no longer intensely opposed. Barrington Moore documents such cases among ascetics, untouchables, and even among some concentration camp victims.[3] When a person's subsistence needs have been denied, he may lose the strength to assert, or even to evaluate, his own interests.[4]

But what do we mean by subsistence needs? While it would clearly be possible to define a brute physiological minimum, there is a compelling case for defining subsistence needs more generously. Let us begin with a notion of the bare minimum:

A *minimum* disaster level is objective in the sense that it represents a food supply close enough to the physiological minimum that further reductions will lead to malnutrition and early death.[5]

There is, of course, some room for cultural variation even in defining this bare minimum. For, as Scott notes, it "assumes a pattern of food preferences." Even compared to the 300 kilos of rice that French geographers once estimated were necessary for Indochinese peasants, "nutritionists have often suggested even cheaper diets which provide the necessary nutrition at a cost in taste which only the very desperate would be willing to pay."[6]

There are important cultural variations between a Thai peasant's notion of rock bottom and the even more meager requirements of a North Vietnamese.[7] Certainly notions of bare subsistence in Western industrialized countries would indicate even more cultural variation. Consider, for example, Orwell's comment on the British unemployment allowances in 1937:

An Englishman on the P.A.C. gets fifteen shillings a week because fifteen shillings is the smallest sum on which he can conceivably keep alive. If he were, say, an Indian or Japanese coolie, who can live on rice and onions, he wouldn't get fifteen shillings a week—he would be lucky if he got fifteen shillings a month. Our unemployment allowances, miserable though they are, are framed to suit a population with very high standards and not much notion of economy.[8]

Similarly, none of the modern subsistence levels calculated by the American or British governments would require a diet so meager as those which are commonly thought sufficient in other parts of the world.[9]

In fact, today's official subsistence levels in Western developed countries are often comparable to diets calculated for the comfortable middle class fifty years earlier. For example, a 1960 subsistence budget in New York City required twice the protein of a 1908 *comfort* budget. The 1960 New York subsistence level was also far more generous in other amenities, such as plumbing facilities, housing, and electric refrigerators.[10]

Hence there are significant cultural variations—both over time and across cultures—in levels of subsistence aimed at some bare level of sufficiency. For even a subsistence level may be provided in widely varying ways depending on the practices of a given culture at a given time.

We might, of course, restrict the notion of subsistence requirements to the limits of physiologically possible (long-term) survival. Or we might arrive at some criterion for more generous, but still minimal, allotments. A plausible version of a more generous requirement was, in fact, formulated in a classic discussion by Adam Smith:

> By necessaries I understand, not only the commodities which are indispensably necessary for the support of life, but whatever the custom of the country renders it *indecent for creditable people, even of the lowest order, to be without.* A linen shirt, for example, is, strictly speaking, not a necessary of life. The Greeks and Romans lived, I suppose, very comfortably, though they had no linen. But in the present times, through the greater part of Europe, a creditable day-labourer would be ashamed to appear in public without a linen shirt. . . . Custom, in the same manner, has rendered leather shoes a necessary of life in England.[11] [Emphasis added.]

He summarizes his criterion as follows: "Under necessaries, therefore, I comprehend, not only those things which nature, but those things which the established rules of decency have rendered necessary to the lowest rank of people."[12]

I propose the lack of the "necessaries" in this sense defined by Adam Smith as a working definition of "disaster" in (i) above. Without the "necessaries" it is either the case that one's very survival is at stake or that one cannot be a "creditable" person "even of the lowest order." One does not then have the opportunity to participate, in a manner compatible with self-esteem (as a "creditable person"), in the life of *any* stratum of the society.[13] If so many options are closed off, then whatever the character of the life plan that results, its development has been influenced by a coercive structure of choice.

Those who are skeptical of this enlarged definition of subsistence[14] may wish to limit the notion to the barest requirements that are physiologically necessary for survival. I believe that this would be a mistake. However, the critique in part 2 of this essay would proceed equally well with either of these definitions. While I propose to employ the more generous notion (Smith's), a skeptical reader may, if he wishes, substitute the barest possible minimum without affecting the essential argument.

Note, however, that in our formulation (i) of a "coercive" structure of choice, we did not require that alternatives actually produce this "disaster" of falling below subsistence. Rather, we required only that every alternative offer a *serious risk* of such disaster. Hence we can formulate the first of two ways in which the "minimal autonomy" of X's life plan can be interfered with as follows:

6. *X's personal life plan has been prevented from developing with even a minimal degree of autonomy*

a. *if it develops within a danger zone in which every alternative offers a serious risk that subsistence needs will not be met.*

By *subsistence needs* I mean those needs that would be satisfied by the "necessaries" in Adam Smith's sense. This (6a) definition is based on the first notion of a coercive structure of choice specified in (i) above. Let us now turn to the second notion, (ii) above, in order to specify a second way in which X's life plan can be prevented from developing with even a minimal degree of autonomy. In that way we will complete definition (6).

The second way in which an individual's choices may be coercively structured occurs when *none* of his options offer him prospects of success. Consider, for example, the life chances of the very poor in the United States. Harrington documents a kind of poverty "constructed so as to destroy aspiration; it is a system designed to be impervious to hope."[15] His comment on the fate of some poor people in a police station is emblematic of their more general fate: "They expected the worst, and they probably got it."[16]

The crucial point is that their life *chances* are extremely limited. As Keniston argues in a similar analysis, a child at the bottom faces "a stacked deck": his odds of doing well are so small—and so obvious—that he comes "to expect failure of himself just as the world expects it of him."[17]

For example, according to a 1974 study: "of every 1,000 children born into the top tenth [of the income distribution] 326 are still there as adults (and many others are not far behind), while only 4 of every 1,000 children born into the bottom tenth ever achieve incomes in the top tenth."[18] In another study, Bowles and Gintis report that if one is born into the bottom tenth in overall socioeconomic background, one has only a 4.2 percent chance of arriving at the top *fifth*.[19] Hence, a few do overcome the odds and achieve great success, but, as Keniston comments, "such miracles occur rarely."[20]

Harrington's famous indictment of conditions in *The Other America* does not overstate the problem: "the real explanation of why the poor are where they are is that they made the mistake of being born to the wrong parents, in the wrong section of the country, in the wrong industry, or in the wrong racial or ethnic group. Once that mistake has been made, they could have been paragons of will and morality but most of them would never even have had a chance to get out of the other America."[21]

Such poor odds coercively structure the development of one's life plan. As noted above, one is taught to "expect failure" by such a "stacked deck." When faced with such odds, the development of their preferences in the first place is decisively influenced by the fact that certain options are, realistically, closed off. The deprivation consists in the coercive character of this structure of options, "constructed," as Harrington says, "so as to destroy aspiration."

Hence a second clause can be added to definition (6) as follows:

6. *X's personal life plan has been prevented from developing with even a minimal degree of autonomy*

a. *if it develops within a danger zone in which every alternative offers a serious risk that subsistence needs will not be met, or*

b. *if X has been denied an adequate life chance, that is, if he experiences remediable conditions such that he cannot realistically aspire to any of the more highly valued positions in the society.*

Several aspects of this definition require more discussion. What do I mean by "any of the more highly valued positions in the society"? What do I mean by "realistically aspire"? And finally, what do I mean by "remediable conditions"?

In any society in which the problem of inadequate life chances arises there will be social inequalities. It will be possible to rank positions in the society according to their desirability—either in terms of a consensus of generally acknowledged rankings or in terms of any of several competing conceptions of those rankings. In the Western industrialized countries there is, apparently, considerable consensus in any given society on the relative desirability of different positions in the society.[22] By *consensus* I mean that there is considerable agreement on these rankings across all sectors of the society. But if there is not such a consensus, it can be assumed that either (a) there are competing conceptions of social inequality operative in the society or (b) there are not social inequalities operative in the society at all.

If (b) is the case, then the question of whether everyone has an adequate life chance does not arise. For in a society with no inequalities, there would be no "more highly valued positions" that some people would be denied the chances to attain. Such a society would be constructed in such a way that it could not impose severe deprivations on some persons by limiting their life chances. Of course other kinds of severe deprivations might still occur. We can set aside this possibility for the moment.[23]

The question of adequate (or inadequate) life chances only arises, then, if there are social inequalities operative in the society. In any such society there will either be a consensus on the character of that hierarchy or there will be competing conceptions. If there is a consensus on the character of the social hierarchy, then by "any of the more highly valued positions" I mean a position regarded as desirable within that hierarchy. This might be operationalized as any position ranked above the median in that hierarchy.

If, instead of consensus, there are competing conceptions, then by "any of the more highly valued positions" I mean a position regarded as desirable within the particular notion of social inequality which that person would choose (if asked, upon reflection, to choose from among the competing conceptions) in order to evaluate his life chances.

In either case, it is required that X have realistic prospects of attaining a position regarded as desirable in terms of notions that are *conventional* within that society. But why should we require that X have the option of conventional success? Suppose he is not interested in the options that are conventionally valued. In that case, how could it count as a deprivation to him if he is prevented from achieving what he does not want?

It should be recalled that we are attempting to define conditions under which it is appropriate for X's preferences to develop in the first place. It is one thing to reject an option one has; it is quite another to reject an option that was always denied. If one never had realistic prospects of attaining *any* of the more (conventionally) desirable positions, then that denial of conventional prospects becomes a coercive influence on the development of one's preferences.

There are two cases of inadequate life chances to be considered. First, there is the case of someone who would, in fact, prize a higher position in the social hierarchy. In this case we face no difficulty in justifying our inference that it could be counted as a benefit to him to have had the chance. Second, there is the case of someone who would not value a higher position. But such a person is in the position of the very poor whose aspirations are destroyed by a "stacked deck." There is considerable evidence that those with limited life prospects learn not to value what they do not have.[24] In coming to expect failure, they quickly learn not to value success. It is in this way that the "stacked deck" has coercively influenced the development of their preferences.

I am not arguing in any sense that people should value success as conventionally defined. I am making the much more limited claim that if they are denied prospects of any success as conventionally defined in their society, then that denial should be considered a coercive influence upon the development of their preferences. It is only in that sense that the denial of a chance, in the first place, constitutes a severe deprivation.

By "realistically aspire" in this definition I mean that the probability of achieving a high position—both as X can subjectively estimate the probability (if X has at least minimal competence) and as we might objectively calculate it—must be above some minimal threshold. There is room for serious debate about the precise line for such a threshold. Skeptics may apply a threshold so minimal as to be without any controversy. Others may be more generous. I only need to assume the application of some such threshold in the argument that follows.

A "remediable condition" is one subject to correction by some policy. Hence if X's life chances are blighted by a congenital defect that cannot be corrected, then X has not been *denied* an adequate life chance. If, however, X's congenital defect subjects him to needless discrimination—which might be corrected by some policy—then the ruin of X's life chances *would* constitute a severe deprivation. If the ruin of X's life chances could also be avoided without any other severe deprivations being imposed, then it would be an instance of tyranny, as well.

In adding these two requirements—that X have an *adequate life chance* and that his *subsistence needs be secure*—I am proposing criteria that are ideal-regarding. For I am claiming that it must count as a severe deprivation to X if he is denied an adequate life chance, or if his subsistence needs are in jeopardy, whether or not X himself protests, opposes, or is even aware of his condition.

Of course X will often, in fact, wish for these minimum requirements to be met. Nevertheless, if he is denied either security for his subsistence needs or an adequate life chance, we are entitled to count those situations as severe deprivations to X whether or not X's actual preferences support our assessment. We thus face the problem of justifying such paternalistic inferences.

One strategy for justifying paternalistic inferences with respect to X would be to claim that X is subject to special *disqualifying conditions* that raise questions about his judgment. There are conditions, in other words, that disqualify X from any claim that his own judgment should be taken as definitive of his interests. For example, there are grounds for overruling a child's judgment (because it is undeveloped), a drunk driver's judgment (because it is clouded by alcohol), or a distraught person's judgment (because it is distorted by duress). In each of these cases there are special conditions that plausibly disqualify X from any claim that his own judgment about his interests should be taken as definitive.[25]

I believe that there is a similar basis for paternalistic judgments if the development of X's preferences has been subjected to either of the coercive conditions specified in this section. Consider our first condition. If X's subsistence needs are denied, he may lose the strength to assert, or even to evaluate, his own interests. If X's subsistence needs are not actually denied, but are, rather, placed at serious risk, all of his other choices will be conditioned by that overriding threat of disaster. In both cases, it is plausible to say that X's preferences—and indeed, the conditions under which his preferences have developed—have been distorted by extreme coercive conditions.

A similar point can be made about our second condition. X's own life plan cannot be taken as definitive of X's own interests if that life plan has been developed under conditions that would not permit him an adequate life chance. If the conditions under which X's preferences develop "destroy aspiration," if they permit him little in the way of hope or of realistic prospects, then we might be permitted a paternalistic judgment even if X himself is fully satisfied.

It is important to note that these disqualifying conditions do not open the floodgate to paternalistic judgments. Rather, they provide a basis for the limited inference that the very conditions that produce the disqualification should be remedied—whether X himself agrees or not. In most cases, of course, X will believe his interests are served by securing his own subsistence needs or by securing at least an adequate life chance. But my point is that these conditions are so fundamental, and their denial so disqualifying, that we would be justified in counting them as severe deprivations whether or not X himself agreed.

They are severe deprivations in the sense provided by our original definition (2). For they are severe deprivations to X because they defeat his personal life plan. They defeat that life plan by preventing it from developing—or at least from developing with even a minimal degree of autonomy.

Now it might be objected that severe deprivations, as they have now been defined, include three different kinds of effects upon a given person X. They include: (a) the extreme reversals to his personal life plan defined in the last chapter, (b) conditions that place his subsistence needs in jeopardy, and (c) conditions that deny him an adequate life chance. As noted, these three effects have in common the fact that, in different ways, they can decisively defeat X's personal plan of life. In that sense, they can each destroy X's essential interests. Nevertheless, it must be admitted that these three kinds of effects are very different. These differences raise the question of whether or not some scheme for comparing them might be worked out.

The question arises, in other words, whether some of these severe deprivations are more "severe" than others. There are two points to be noted about such a possibility. First, while such a scheme would be desirable in a more complete theory, it would also, in principle, face more extreme versions of the twin difficulties we have been exploring at length here—the problem of making interpersonal comparisons for want-regarding claims and the problem of justifying paternalistic inferences for ideal-regarding claims. While neither of these difficulties should be regarded as insuperable, they both should be regarded as posing formidable challenges—challenges that, I believe, have been met thus far, within the limited sphere of my proposal.

The second and more important point about this possibility is that its difficulties are entirely avoided by the definition proposed here. For the definition of simple tyranny requires no such comparisons. That definition leaves entirely open the question of how severe deprivations are to be compared. Remember that a policy is only classified as tyrannous when an alternative policy would not impose *any* severe deprivations—in any of these three senses—on anyone. The only comparisons required are between (1) severe deprivations in any of these three senses and (2) other kinds of effects. The *relative* severity of deprivations under (1) is never an issue.

At this point it might be useful to summarize the account of severe deprivations and tyranny offered, thus far, over the last several chapters:

1. *A policy choice by the government is an instance of simple tyranny when that policy imposes severe deprivations even though an alternative policy would have imposed no severe deprivations on anyone.*

2. *A severe deprivation is the destruction of an essential interest.*

3. *X's personal life plan is the constellation of private-regarding wants and courses of action to which he is committed.*

4. *A severe deprivation to X is the decisive defeat of X's personal life plan.*

5. *X's personal life plan has been decisively defeated*

a. *if it is prevented from ever developing with even a minimal degree of autonomy, or*

b. *if portions of it encounter reversals so important to X that X could not be fully compensated by the fulfillment of any of his other private-regarding preferences.*

6. *X's personal life plan has been prevented from developing with even a minimal degree of autonomy*

a. *if it develops within a danger zone in which every alternative offers a serious risk that subsistence needs will not be met, or*

b. *if X has been denied an adequate life chance, that is, if he experiences remediable conditions such that he cannot realistically aspire to any of the more highly valued positions in the society.*

6. Causality, Risk, and Alternative Policies

In the last several chapters I have focused on the notion of severe deprivations. There are some other aspects of the definition of simple tyranny that also require clarification. What does it mean to say that a policy "imposes" a severe deprivation when an "alternative policy" would not? These notions require a discussion of four related topics: (a) causality, (b) the foreseeability of consequences, (c) risk, and (d) policy alternatives.

The relations among these topics can be seen from the following two definitions:

7. *A policy imposes a severe deprivation if it can be reasonably foreseen to be connected to consequences that constitute that severe deprivation.*

8. *A policy is connected to consequences if it causally produces or fails to causally prevent those consequences.*

If Amin orders the expulsion of the Asians, that order causally produces severe deprivations. If, on the other hand, they starve—when that starvation could clearly have been prevented—then the failure to prevent their starvation imposes severe deprivations. In either case, a policy is connected, in a reasonably foreseeable way, to consequences that constitute severe deprivations.

From (8) we require a notion of causality; from (7) we require a discussion of consequences being "reasonably foreseen"; this notion, in turn, carries us into a discussion of risk. And lastly, it is the notion of severe deprivations being "imposed" that permits us to define "policy alternatives."

Causal statements about the consequences of a government policy are obviously complicated by the fact that many of those consequences are themselves human actions. This same complexity applies, of course, to notions of causality employed in the law. I believe that we may usefully borrow from the account of causality in the law developed by Hart and Honoré.[1]

They distinguish three notions of causality employed in legal reasoning. First, there is what they call the "central concept," most obviously applicable to connections among physical events. The "central concept" is "a contingency, usually a human intervention, which initiates a series of physical changes, which exemplify connexions between types of event; and its features are best seen in the simplest cases of all where a human being manipulates things in order to bring about intended change."[2]

But in many of the cases that will concern us, the immediate consequences of a policy should not be understood as a "physical change" or a "series of physical changes."[3] Rather, that immediate consequence may be the influence upon some person or group to perform actions that may, in turn, have consequences that constitute severe deprivations (or those persons' actions may influence other persons who, in turn, perform actions, and so on).

In order to deal with such cases, Hart and Honoré add two other notions of causality to the central concept. We will do the same. These additional species of causation are, first, that A may "cause" B to perform an act by providing him with a "reason," and, second, that A may "cause" B to perform an act by providing him with an "opportunity."

Consider these examples of A influencing B by providing him with a "reason": "He made me do it," "He persuaded me to do it," "He induced me to do it," "I did it because he offered me a reward," "I did it because he threatened me."[4] In all of these cases the first actor intentionally influences the second to perform an action by "providing a motive"[5] (or by activating a motive that was preexisting, for example, B's wish for money, which was activated when he was offered a reward). It should be obvious that a government may impose severe deprivations by "providing a reason" for individuals to perform actions that, in turn, have consequences that constitute severe deprivations.

One person provides another "with a reason" when he "does or says something with the intention that it should appear to the other as a reason for doing something."[6] However, there are cases in which one person influences another to perform an action without the first person having any *intention* of bringing about the action on the part of the second. The first person may bring about a state of affairs that provides the second with an "opportunity": "A man who carelessly leaves unlocked the doors of a house, entrusted to him by a friend, has provided the thief with an opportunity."[7] In this enlarged sense of causality, the failure to provide an opportunity may also have important consequences: "The failure of a government to send general reinforcements is held to have been the cause of a defeat."[8]

Each of these three notions will be treated as varieties of causality in definitions (7) and (8) above: (a) causality in the sense of connections between physical events susceptible to general (law-like) explanations, (b) causality in the sense of providing a "reason" for an action, and (c) causality in the sense of providing an "opportunity" for an action.

Now in each of these cases, the issue is not whether a government policy *actually* is causally connected to a given severe deprivation. Rather, the issue is whether it is "reasonably foreseeable" that the policy will have such effects.

The evaluation of a given policy should proceed, in other words, in terms of those effects that can be reasonably foreseen rather than in terms of those effects that actually result. For the problem of policy choice is posed in terms of the effects that can be foreseen. If a criterion, such as the principle that tyranny is to be avoided, is to be prescriptive, then it must be appropriate to apply that criterion to situations of actual choice.

This is, of course, a general problem for moral theory. Feinberg offers a compelling example that concerns individual moral choice:

> If a householder invites a passing stranger to come in from the rain and take shelter on his covered porch, and the stranger is hit by lightning as he passes a tree near the house (L. Garvin, *A Modern Introduction to Ethics,* p. 233), we would naturally say that the householder did the right thing in offering the stranger shelter, but that his proper conduct has unforeseeably disastrous consequences; *not* that the householder acted wrongly (but blamelessly) in tendering the invitation.[9] [Italics in original.]

It was reasonably foreseeable that the stranger would be benefited by the offer of shelter; the offer should be evaluated in terms of those foreseen consequences rather than in terms of the unexpected disaster that actually resulted. I take a similar position with respect to connections among policies and severe deprivations.

But what counts as "reasonably foreseeable"? Those consequences are reasonably foreseeable which may be expected with confidence after a knowledgeable and impartial assessment of the available facts. This formula raises two questions: How "knowledgeable" about the facts should such an assessment be? What do we mean by "impartial"?

Consider a case where A does not actually foresee certain consequences, and, based on the information he has available to him, those consequences cannot be predicted. Nevertheless, it might still be the case that those consequences were reasonably foreseeable. For one may be held responsible not only for what may be predicted on the basis of what one knows, but also for what may be predicted on the basis of what one *should have known*. What A is ignorant about—when he should not have been —could have provided a basis for consequences being foreseen even if they could not be foreseen on the basis of A's actual state of knowledge at the time.

G. E. M. Anscombe offers the example of a ship's pilot (who should have known about certain navigational obstacles) and a cook (who should have known that salt was necessary for the potatoes). In each case we may say that their "ignorance is voluntary."[10] They can be held responsible for not knowing; we might say that "they should have known better." Their ignorance is voluntary because "when it was necessary and possible for the pilot to navigate and for the cook to put salt in the potatoes, the loss of the ship and the spoiling of the potatoes are ascribed to the pilot and cook as causes. . . . So when it was necessary and possible for A to know, the ignorance is ascribed to A's will as cause."[11]

This sense of "necessary" is the instrumental one, meaning that something is required for a given end ("Things are in this sense necessary when without them some good can't be got or some evil avoided.").[12] We might add to this the requirement that the end for which the information is necessary must be worth the effort of acquiring the information. For the costs of the information might be so great as to outweigh the end gained by the information. The decision to invest in the effort to secure information must itself be subjected to assessment based on its probable payoffs in light of what is already known. But with these qualifications, Anscombe's notion of "voluntary ignorance" should be included within the notion of "reasonably foreseeable consequences" in this way: Consequences are reasonably foreseeable not only when they can be foreseen on the basis of the knowledge one actually has, but also when they can be foreseen on the basis of the knowledge one is "voluntarily ignorant" about (that is, the knowledge one should have had).

The definition above required that the assessment of "reasonably foreseeable consequences" be both knowledgeable and impartial. By this I mean that the causal connections that are expected with confidence are those that would be supported by scientific (including social scientific) inquiry.[13] This means, of course, that there are severe limits on the causal connections that can be invoked in any claim that severe deprivations will result from a policy.

Two points should be made about this requirement. First, it is a specification of conditions for the application of a moral principle, with a high degree of confidence, to special situations. It is not a prescription for routine policy analysis. I am not claiming, in other words, that every choice among alternative policies should turn on a scientific assessment of the facts. That would clearly be an enormously wasteful way to distribute scarce resources for scientific (and social scientific) research. Rather, I am claiming that when the special issue of tyranny arises, any claim that severe deprivations will result from a policy should be subjected to special, critical scrutiny. And because such a claim necessarily involves causal inferences (that is, that severe deprivations will result from a given policy and that no severe deprivations will result from some alternative policy), these causal inferences should be subject to examination in terms of practices suitable for the critical scrutiny of causal inferences. These practices I take to be those of scientific inquiry (from both the physical and social sciences).

This position raises a second issue. Some persons may *believe* that they will suffer severe deprivations because they accept certain causal inferences that are not subject to scientific support. Consider, for example, a religious sect whose members believe that if *others* persist in disturbing the tranquility of the Sabbath, *they* (the members of the sect) will be denied salvation. Or, in another variation, everyone will suffer because the coming of the Messiah will be delayed.[14] In this case the severe deprivation consists in a future state of affairs (the denial of salvation to the group or the delay of the Messiah) that is allegedly connected in a causal way to certain present actions of others. The difficulty is that the alleged causal connections are entirely beyond scientific assessment.

Even plausible principles, when combined with implausible facts, can produce absurd conclusions. While there are sometimes difficulties in distinguishing those disputes that are factual from those that are value-laden,[15] it is useful, nevertheless, to separate the two for certain analytic purposes.

Any application of the principle of nontyranny depends on a picture of the facts. Because the relevant facts turn on certain causal inferences, it seems reasonable to require that these causal inferences stand up to scientific assessment. A skeptic might wish to apply more permissive criteria to alleged causal connections. While this would, in my judgment, be a mistake, it would not affect the central argument presented in part 2 (although it would obviously affect some particular examples already discussed[16]).

It should be noted that there is an important difference between (a) a scientific assessment of a causal connection that X believes and (b) a scientific assessment that X believes in a causal connection (however dubious that connection). There are important cases where a claim about a severe deprivation will depend on an assessment of the (b) kind rather than of the (a) kind. In this way, causal connections that are scientifically unsupportable will play an important role in inferences about severe deprivations.

Consider, for example, members of a tribe such as the Yoruba, who believe that in little wooden boxes they are carrying their "souls."[17] There is the story of certain anthropologists who attempted to demonstrate to the Yoruba that their "souls" were not contained in the wooden boxes. They arranged a scientific experiment: before a suitable audience they smashed one of the boxes. The result was that the tribesman whose box they smashed fell dead on the spot.[18]

We can infer that the Yoruba tribesman suffered a severe deprivation (from shock, or a heart attack, or some other physiological reaction) without our having to accept the Yoruba's scientifically dubious causal claim that his "soul" was destroyed when the box was smashed. For we can infer, rather, that he suffered a severe deprivation because he *believed* in that dubious causal connection. The role that his belief played in the actually operative causal connections is itself susceptible to scientific investigation. We could accept that his dubious belief was a necessary condition for his reaction without also accepting the content of the belief. In this way, causal propositions that are not scientifically supportable may, nevertheless, have to be considered in a scientific assessment of the causal connections that produce severe deprivations.

Another problem about the "reasonable foreseeability" of deprivations concerns the availability of information to those directly affected. This difficulty arises because many of the severe deprivations discussed here are want regarding, that is, they are defined in terms of the actual preferences of the persons affected. Suppose that the government can foresee that group X will consider certain consequences to be severe deprivations provided they know about those consequences. Can the government avoid tyranny by simply suppressing or falsifying the relevant information?

I believe that except for two possibilities that require special treatment, this objection is misplaced. For normally it will not be possible for X to experience a severe deprivation of the want-regarding kind and not be aware of that fact. In other words, it will not be possible for him to experience a decisive reversal to his personal life plan and not know it (at least eventually).[19]

We must distinguish, however: (1) X being aware of his severe deprivation, and (2) X being aware in addition that his severe deprivation can be attributed to some government policy. There may be ample room for a government to manipulate information so as to keep X from the second kind of knowledge. But this means only that the government is attempting the kind of cover-up that will make its policy *appear* nontyrannous. Such a policy will be tyrannous all the same.

It is, of course, true that severe deprivations must be connected to some government policy or other before a claim of tyranny can be substantiated. It may be easy to mislead an impartial inquiry into believing that certain severe deprivations cannot be attributed to *any* policy. Investigators might be led, for example, to attribute them to natural causes when they really resulted from government policy or government negligence. Imagine, for example, a cover-up involving the continued use of a potent carcinogen whose properties are not publicly known. It would be easy to wrongly attribute the results of such a policy to natural causes. These, however, are problems of application rather than of definition.

The two possibilities that require special treatment are (1) deprivations that involve, as one of their consequences, an impairment to X's *ability* to evaluate his interests, and (2) *risks* that do not eventuate in actual harm.

Suppose that X is subjected to consequences that impair or destroy his reasoning ability or that, say, affect his sanity. He may then have experienced a decisive reversal to the life plan in progress at the time of the impairment, but he may have been rendered incapable of realizing it. To dramatize the situation slightly, a cover-up by the government that substance Z has such physiological effects may prevent the people involved —and anyone else—from ever realizing that severe deprivations have been imposed by government policies.

In such a case we might posit that a paternalistic judgment on behalf of X is required. More specifically, when a deprivation consists in an impairment to X's ability to know that he has suffered a severe deprivation, then an inference is required about the conclusion X *would* have drawn about his own condition were he to judge with the abilities he had before the impairment. Such an inference would, of course, be difficult in practice. But it is required only for special conditions. We do not encounter any such cases in the arguments that follow.[20]

Let us now turn to the question of risks. We said earlier that policies had to be evaluated in terms of the causal connections that were reasonably foreseeable. What if severe deprivations that were reasonably foreseeable later fail to result? If there was an alternative policy that would not involve any severe deprivations, then would the choice of the risky policy be tyrannous—even if the risk of severe deprivations resulted in no actual harm? Note that it is even possible for X to be exposed to a serious risk and never know it. Suppose that an oil storage depot near X nearly blew up. If the risk did not actually issue in disaster, X might never know.

I will adopt a suggestion of Nozick's that a *risk* of harm, if sufficiently serious, should be treated as an actual harm—whether or not it eventuates in any harm at all. Consider his example of being forced to play Russian roulette.[21] If I am forced to play with, say, a one-in-five chance of being shot (one of the gun's five chambers is loaded), I would have grounds for extremely serious objections, whether or not I was actually shot. Another way of saying this is that the harm is reasonably expectable even though it does not actually result.

Of course, there are important difficulties about how severe such a risk must be if it is to count as an actual harm.[22] Suppose, to pursue Nozick's example, that there are 100,000 chambers in the gun (or, in another words, that the gun is constructed so that there is only one chance in 100,000 that it will go off). At some point, risks clearly become insignificant and cannot be treated as actual harms. For the conduct of any activity presumes some "background" level of risk.[23] These must be differentiated from serious risks, in general, and serious risks involving severe deprivations, in particular.

Note further that this way of treating risks avoids the difficulty mentioned before. For we can judge that X was exposed to a serious risk without X himself having to know that he was exposed to such a risk. Once again, while government manipulation of information might affect whether a policy *appears* tyrannous, it would not affect the substance of whether it was tyrannous.

We have now discussed causality, the foreseeability of consequences, and risk. We have remaining a set of issues that concerns the definition of policy alternatives.

Imagine a state of affairs in which severe deprivations to Y are unavoidable. Does this mean that every possible policy must be credited with the severe deprivation to Y? This would mean that our principle (that simple tyranny is to be avoided) could be easily trivialized. For if every alternative can so easily involve a severe deprivation, then avoiding simple tyranny will prescribe nothing whatsoever (for there would then be no alternatives that avoided severe deprivations).

The difficulty can be avoided once the meaning of *alternative policies* is clarified. Consider this definition:

9. *Policy A_1 is an alternative to policy A_2 if the severe deprivations that would be imposed by A_1 differ from those that would be imposed by A_2.*

I mean to include within this definition the case of an alternative imposing no severe deprivations at all. So if A_1 imposes no severe deprivations, that would, of course, define it as a policy alternative distinct from a policy A_2 that imposes severe deprivations.

It might be objected that this definition does not sufficiently distinguish among policies in two cases: (a) the case where policies all impose no severe deprivations, and (b) the case where policies all impose precisely the same deprivations (perhaps through different causal mechanisms).

It is true that in both of these cases definition (9) would not differentiate such policies as distinct alternatives. However, neither of these differentiations is necessary for any application of our definition of simple tyranny. For if two policies impose precisely the same severe deprivations, then choosing either policy must be equally tyrannous, or nontyrannous, depending on whether there is *another* alternative that would impose no deprivations. Similarly, if two policies both impose no deprivations, then choosing either policy must be equally nontyrannous—and may, indeed, be required if there is *another* alternative that would impose severe deprivations. Hence the fact that these policies are not distinguished can never make a difference in an application of our definition of simple tyranny. So for our purposes, this definition should suffice.

How does this resolve our initial difficulty? Note that by definition (7), a policy *imposes* a severe deprivation when it is reasonably foreseen to be *connected to* consequences that constitute that deprivation. A severe deprivation that is unavoidable cannot be connected to every new policy.

For every new policy did not causally produce those consequences, nor did every new policy fail to causally prevent those consequences. A policy fails to causally prevent consequences when it does not succeed in preventing them—when they were *preventable*. Consequences that are preventable at one time may not be preventable at another.

Hence if there is a severe deprivation to Y that persists unavoidably, that would not define a deprivation that should be credited to every policy. For it would not be "connected," in the relevant sense, to every policy. By our definition, that deprivation would only be credited to the policies that *imposed* it. Other policies, similarly, would only be credited with the severe deprivation they were causally connected to. Once policy alternatives are distinguished in this way, the apparent trivialization of simple tyranny is avoided.

Now consider another difficulty with the definition of policy alternatives. How is the nexus of alternative policies to be defined in any given case? We may certainly imagine disagreements about the consequences of possible policies and about the range of possibilities that one person or another might envisage.

For any application of the definition of tyranny proposed here this is, of course, a crucial question. For a policy that imposes severe deprivations is only classified as tyrannous when an alternative policy would impose no severe deprivations on anyone.

A policy is said to impose severe deprivations when its causal connection to those deprivations is reasonably foreseeable. Just as a policymaker can only be held responsible for the consequences that could have been foreseen at the time of the choice, based on the information available, so he can only be held responsible for the *alternatives* that were reasonably foreseeable at the time—based on the kind of scientific knowledge of causal connections available at that time.[24] If, for example, the economic theories available were primitive so that he could not have known that his policies would produce massive unemployment, we cannot say that his policies "imposed" the unemployment merely because we *later* develop a theory that plausibly explains the connection.

So just as the definition of severe deprivations imposed by a policy depends on a scientific assessment of causal alternatives, so does the definition of policy alternatives depend on a scientific assessment of the causal connections. A_1 is a policy alternative to A_2 if an impartial analysis of causal connections leads to the conclusion that the severe deprivations that would be imposed by A_1 differ from those that would be imposed by

A_2. Just as dubious causal connections should not be included in the definition of the severe deprivations imposed by a given policy, they also should not be included in the definition of the alternatives to a given policy.

But how is our scientific assessment of policy alternatives ever to be completed? As Lindblom has persuasively argued, for most problems it would be irrational for a policymaker to attempt to "synoptically" consider *all* of the possibilities. For many problems the list of possibilities cannot, in principle, be completed. Furthermore, attempts simply to enlarge the list of possibilities would often encounter enormous information costs.[25]

But these attempts seem to be required by our proposal. For if every apparent policy alternative would impose severe deprivations, are we not then required to continue the search for alternatives as long as there is some possibility that a nondeprivating alternative will be identified? Enormous resources would then be perpetually tied up in tasks of policy analysis that might, in principle, be beyond completion.

The decision to invest in a search to enlarge the nexus of alternative policies (the list of possible choices that are already reasonably foreseeable, based on the information at hand) is itself a policy choice. That policy choice, like any other, has to be evaluated in terms of its probable consequences. A further search for new possibilities is *only* required if there is already reason to believe that there are good prospects that a nondeprivating alternative will be revealed.

For just as a high risk of a severe deprivation should be treated as an actual severe deprivation (for purposes of policy choice), a high probability that severe deprivations will be avoided should be treated as the actual avoidance of deprivations (for purposes of policy choice). Only when the probability is high enough that a nontyrannous alternative will be revealed is a further search for alternatives then required by our definition of tyranny. What, precisely, counts as a high (or low) risk of harm or probability of benefit will not be settled here. Rather, I only need to assume, in principle, that such thresholds can be defined in order to argue that this difficulty can be avoided. Further searches that are unlikely to pay off are not required by the principle.

Now that we have defined alternative policies, risk, and the imposition of severe deprivations, we are, at long last, at the point where these definitions can be applied in a critique of political principles. The strategy of that critique, however, remains to be explained.

7. The Critique of Ultimate Criteria

Avoiding simple tyranny is proposed here as a necessary condition for morally acceptable principles. A principle that would justify imposing severe deprivations—when an alternative policy would have imposed no severe deprivations on anyone—is defective as an ideal that can legitimately prescribe social choices.

But what kinds of principles, precisely, should be subjected to this test? I should say something about the general class of criteria for which this condition is being proposed.

I propose to apply this condition to what might be called *ultimate criteria* for social choice. Ultimate criteria purport to resolve the moral questions to which they apply without having to be balanced against other considerations. Their implications are clearly specifiable; they are not tempered by clauses such as "other things being equal" or *"ceteris paribus."* Ultimate criteria have another important characteristic: they assume relatively favorable conditions. They are offered as ideals to be aspired to when conditions are encouraging; they are not offered as remedies for injustice when conditions are cruel and limiting. Conditions of the latter kind might require us to "think the unthinkable" and to violate one important principle in order to preserve another.[1] Under such dreadful limitations it might be easy to criticize almost any principle. For example, in a "triage" situation in which someone must be sacrificed, it may be the case that no solution is beyond reproach. But the conditions presumed by ultimate criteria are more optimistic. It is only on this chosen ground (under such relatively favorable conditions) that our critique of various ultimate criteria will be applied. If under these conditions a criterion would legitimate tyranny, then it must be rejected.

Let me formulate these ground rules more precisely. I will say that a principle is an *ultimate criterion* for social choice if it satisfies two requirements: (1) it must be formulated so as to apply to *ideal theory;* and (2) it must conform to the logic of *strong principles.*

Each of these conditions requires more explanation. I take the term "ideal theory" from Rawls.[2] Drawing on his account, let us say that a principle applies to ideal theory if it prescribes social choices when two conditions hold: (a) conditions are relatively favorable; and (b) people can generally be assumed to comply with the principles proposed.

By "relatively favorable conditions" I mean, first of all, what Rawls calls "moderate scarcity": "Natural and other resources are not so abundant that schemes of cooperation become superfluous, nor are conditions so harsh that fruitful ventures must inevitably break down."[3] We might specify the lower limit more precisely by saying that conditions must be sufficiently favorable that it is possible to rule out the "danger zone" to subsistence needs (it is possible to ensure the "necessaries" discussed in chapter 5) for everyone.

But there is another important sense in which I assume conditions to be favorable. By "relatively favorable" I also mean that the conditions under which the principle applies are not, themselves, primarily the result of previous violations of the proposed theory. Rawls argues, quite rightly, that "partial compliance theory" poses special problems.[4] If the existing conditions are themselves the result of previous violations of the principle being considered, special problems result. If, in other words, a status quo has been created through tyranny, injustice, or oppression, special difficulties are encountered in the attempt to fully implement a principle in a situation that has been brought about through such violations. Many plausible principles would encounter this problem in, say, Rhodesia, South Africa, or Northern Ireland at the present time.

Even our own proposed criterion of nontyranny would require some effort at adaptation to such situations. Imagine an ongoing system of slavery that has been erected and maintained by tyrannous action. Should the slaveholders be protected from the economic hardship that would result from emancipation? If the slaves are freed, must the owners be compensated?

It should be clear that if the entire economic system is done away with, the slaveholders' way of life may be destroyed to such an extent that the reversal would appear to constitute, in some cases, a severe deprivation according to our proposed definition in chapter 4. However, their advantaged position is, itself, primarily the result of violations of the principle. It is precisely the special problems of this kind of situation that fall outside of ideal theory.

In speculating about how to apply the definition of tyranny outside the bounds of ideal theory, we might add the following requirement: If the status quo with respect to which a severe deprivation is claimed is itself primarily the result of simple tyranny—within the lifetime of the person advantaged—then those advantages of tyranny do not serve as the appropriate status quo for defining severe deprivations. For that person's complicity in the tyrannous policies may be regarded as disqualifying him from any claim that the status quo is the appropriate benchmark for comparison.[5] Rather, some complex counterfactual assessment about how well off one *would* have been—were it not for the advantages from tyrannous policies —would be required.

It should be obvious that such counterfactual assessments pose great difficulties. These difficulties, however, fall within the purview of *nonideal* theory. We do not need to deal with any of them here, for it is only within the simplifying assumptions of ideal theory that our argument proceeds.

In ideal theory, conditions can thus be assumed to be relatively favorable in two senses: first, conditions no more severe than moderate scarcity obtain; second, those conditions are not themselves primarily the result of previous violations of the principle being considered.

In addition, following Rawls, we may assume continuing "strict compliance." People can generally be assumed to comply with the proposed principles. At the time when principles are implemented there is, thus, a great deal of social cooperation that can be assumed.

Ideal theory thus involves some extremely optimistic assumptions. It does not presume to prescribe choices when conditions are so harsh that all the choices are relatively unfavorable. Triage situations, "tragic choices,"[6] and remedies for previous injustice all lie outside its scope. Similarly, when there is less than full social cooperation in implementing a principle, then "strict compliance" no longer obtains.

The conditions of ideal theory are, however, not utopian; they might, in fact, be implemented in some real (and fortunate) societies. Such a theory is also relevant to other societies in offering an ideal to be aspired to—a social vision that cannot, for the moment, be fulfilled, but that may, nevertheless, be approached.

Principles may also, of course, apply within nonideal theory. But they have to apply within ideal theory to be classified as "ultimate criteria" here. It is only within ideal theory—it is only their adequacy as ideals under these optimistic assumptions—that I shall criticize here. If a principle would legitimate simple tyranny even when such fortunate conditions obtain, then it must be unacceptable as an ideal for social choice.

That a principle apply to ideal theory was only one of the two characteristics of what I called an "ultimate criterion." An ultimate criterion must also conform to the logic of strong principles. This amounts to saying that the principle must have specifiable and determinate implications. A brief digression may be required to explain this requirement.

Borrowing from David Lyons, we may distinguish two components of any moral principle: a requirement for action "r" and some prerequisites or conditions (under which that requirement holds) "p." For example, a strong principle that promises should be kept might require that I do something (r) under the condition that I have promised it (p). Such a strong principle then has the logical structure:

If p, then r.[7]

If certain conditions obtain (p), then a requirement for action (r) follows. If I have promised something (p), then I should do it (r).

Any principle with clearly specifiable implications can be represented by this logical structure. "P" and "r" may, of course, be quite complex, but the point remains the same. As long as the conditions for "p" are spelled out so that we can determine when "p" obtains, then the connection to the requirement for action "r" is simple and, indeed, logically unavoidable. When the connection between "p" and "r" is strong in this way, the principle may be referred to as a "strong" principle.

There is, however, another way in which principles have frequently been formulated. In these cases, the connection between "p" and "r" is not strong. Rather, it is complicated by a phrase such as "other things being equal" or *"ceteris paribus."* In such cases, we may find ourselves in the position of knowing that "p" (whatever prerequisities have been specified) fully obtains, but not knowing whether a requirement for action follows (from p conjoined with the principle). For such a requirement only follows when "p" obtains *and* "other things" are equal. The extra clause performs the role of an additional but unspecifiable prerequisite. The logic of such principles has the form:

If p and q, then r.[8]

If "p" obtains but "q" does not, no conclusion whatsoever about what should be done then follows. Given such a principle, we could know that I had promised something (p), but we would not be entitled to conclude that I should do it (r). For no conclusion follows until we know about "q" —until we know whether or not "other things are equal."

Such principles are called "weak" or *prima facie* principles.[9] They are weak because the connection between "p" and "r" is weakened by the addition of "q"—the *"ceteris paribus"* or "other things being equal" clause among the prerequisites for action. "P" might obtain: I might have promised something, but if the principle of keeping promises is weak, then I am not required to keep the promise *unless* "other things are equal."

If the conditions could be specified under which it would be concluded that the "q" ("other things being equal") clause is fulfilled, then those conditions could be built into the definition of "p" (or into a revised version of "p"). In other words, some apparently weak principles can be reformulated into strong principles once the "q" clause is sufficiently clarified. Such principles might be quite complicated, but they would be strong in form nevertheless. It is only when the weakening clause resists precise specification that the principle should be classified as weak. Such principles produce an ethical position that requires that principles be "balanced" one against another according to no specifiable weights or determinate formula. For if the weights were specified, then, of course, a new strong principle could be determined. If, for example, precise indifference curves could be drawn, then these would determine a new strong principle. But when the balancing of principles cannot be adequately captured by some formula, the result is that they must be balanced by "intuition."

Rawls aptly calls the resulting position "intuitionism." It is the position "that there exist no higher-order constructive criteria for determining the proper emphasis for the competing principles."[10] A balance must be struck in a way that cannot be clearly specified; in this way the choice must, in the end, be left to "intuition." In this sense intuitionism is not an alternative theory but the absence of a theory.[11]

Ultimate criteria of the kind we will examine must be "strong" in form. This is merely the requirement that their implications be specified. They determine conditions under which, it is claimed, certain choices should be made, and they are logically formulated so that when those conditions obtain there is no ambiguity about whether they would require those choices.

All of the criteria we shall examine have been offered as ultimate criteria in this dual sense: they are strong principles that apply to ideal theory. They assume the optimistic conditions of ideal theory and then clearly specify certain choices under those conditions. In the chapters that follow I argue that under those optimistic conditions they would clearly specify choices that include simple tyranny in the sense defined here. This is their decisive theoretical defect.

Now there are two ways in which a principle can clearly specify a choice that counts as simple tyranny. Recall that tyranny has been defined here as the choice of a policy (say A_1) that imposes severe deprivations when an alternative policy (say A_2) would impose no severe deprivations on anyone. A principle legitimates tyranny if it justifies or supports the choice of A_1 rather than A_2. It may do this in either of two ways: (1) by prescribing A_1 rather than A_2, or (2) by rating them as equally good.[12] In either case, were a government to choose A_1 rather than A_2 it could invoke the given principle in support of its decision. In case (1) it could claim that it was required by the principle to choose A_1. In case (2) it could claim that according to the given principle, A_2 is at least as good as A_1. Hence it cannot be criticized, on moral grounds, for choosing one rather than the other. For the fact that they are rated as equally good (or, stated in another way, that moral *indifference* is prescribed between A_1 and A_2) means that there is no moral issue at stake in the choice of one rather than the other. We *could not be wrong* in choosing one rather than the other.

These two possibilities must be clearly distinguished from a third: namely, the situation where the given principle says *nothing* about how A_1 and A_2 are to be compared. For in that case the principle cannot be invoked in support of a given choice. For the principle will then have been formulated in such a way that it does not apply to that particular case at all. There is, then, a crucial difference between silence and indifference: between saying nothing and saying that two alternatives are equally good.

In the arguments that follow, principles will be criticized because they would support tyrannous choices in either of the two ways ([1] and [2]) just specified. My argument will be that such principles must be inadequate because they violate our proposed necessary condition.

Nontyranny has been proposed here as a necessary condition for an ultimate criterion to be morally acceptable. Any principle that legitimates simple tyranny should be rejected as inadequate. This does *not* mean, of course, that any principle that satisfies this minimal test should be accepted. We have proposed a *necessary* but not sufficient condition. It is only a minimal test.

From this limited claim, it does not even follow that any principle that legitimates simple tyranny is worse than any principle that does not. Suppose I claimed that an acceptable plan for survival in the desert must include provisions for water. Such provisions would be a necessary condition for an acceptable plan. But this would not mean that *any* plan that did not provide for water was worse than *any* plan that did not. For consider another plan, one that did not include provisions for *food*. Provisions for food might also be reasonably considered a necessary condition (for an acceptable plan). We could maintain our claim that provision for water was a necessary condition without being committed to any claim comparing a plan with food but no water with another plan with water but no food. These two plans might, for example, be equally bad. Or the one without food might be even worse. All that we can conclude from the claim that provision for water is a necessary condition for an acceptable plan is that when a plan fails this test it must be rejected as unacceptable.

Similarly, nontyranny has been proposed here as a necessary but not a sufficient condition for an acceptable principle. If a principle violates that necessary condition, then it must be rejected. But this proposed test does not presume to exhaust the grounds upon which principles may be rejected. It is possible for a principle to pass this test but have some other defect that is just as bad (or perhaps even worse). It may, in other words, provide for water but not for food.

Only one claim follows from the proposal: if a principle does in fact fail the test—if it would legitimate the choices defined here as simple tyranny—then it should be rejected. For then it is not a morally acceptable ideal for prescribing social choices. Like a plan for survival that lacks provision for water, it is unacceptable. It is only this test, based merely on the claim that nontyranny is a necessary condition for acceptable principles, that is directed at the principles in Part Two.

Part Two. Tyranny and Alternative Principles

8. Procedural Principles

In the chapters that follow I offer critiques of three general kinds of principles for social choice. In each case my argument is that because these criteria would legitimate tyranny, they are defective as ultimate ideals for social choice. Of course, I do not mean to deny that these criteria identify important moral considerations; they may play, for example, the role of *prima facie* principles in any social choice. As "weak" criteria, they may have an important place. But as "ultimate criteria," which are to be applied without exceptions or qualifications, they are inadequate.

I do not claim that all of the particular arguments that follow are original or surprising. Some of the citations should indicate those that are already well known. I do believe, however, that the overall result is a new contribution: that all principles of these three general kinds should be rejected as ultimate criteria because they would legitimate tyranny in the sense proposed here.

The first argument is directed at procedural principles. As noted in chapter 1, a procedural principle is one that specifies a rule of decision but that specifies nothing about the content of those decisions—apart from possible requirements that the rule of decision not be altered in the future.[1] By a *rule of decision* I mean a specification that support (that is, agreement, concurrence, or actions of assent) from certain combinations of persons (that is, certain numbers, proportions, or particular groups of persons, perhaps in some specified order) is necessary and sufficient to produce authoritative (that is, legitimate) actions by the regime.

As long as a criterion leaves open the possibility that *anything* may be done—provided it has support from the persons or groups specified by the decision rule—it is procedural in the proposed sense. Criteria that would define legitimate political regimes as those preserving consent or unanimity or majority rule or political equality (conjoined with a specific decision rule) offer examples of procedural criteria.

Precisely because my argument is meant to apply generally to all procedural principles, I am not able to do justice to the enormous differences among procedural principles. I am only able to discuss difficulties that result from an important feature they have in common.

I first consider procedural principles that have nonunanimous rules of decision, that is, rules of decision that do not require the support or agreement of everyone. I then turn to the case of unanimous decision rules. In both cases my argument proceeds within the bounds of ideal theory. Following my discussion in the last chapter, I assume: (1) that everyone supports the proposed procedural principle (there is "strict compliance") and (2) that conditions are favorable in that (a) conditions of only "moderate scarcity" obtain and (b) the situation in which the proposed procedural principle is applied is not itself primarily the result of past violations of the principle. All of these optimistic assumptions are compatible with the argument that follows. Because procedural principles would legitimate simple tyranny under these optimistic assumptions, they must be defective as ultimate criteria.

My argument in this chapter can be regarded as a generalization to *all* procedural principles of Schumpeter's famous argument against one particular procedural principle—majoritarian democracy. To support his claim that democracy should not be considered an ethical "end in itself," Schumpeter invites us to participate in "a mental experiment":

Suppose that a community, in a way which satisfies the reader's criteria of democracy, reached the decision to persecute religious dissent. The instance is not fanciful. Communities which most of us would readily recognize as democracies have burned heretics at the stake—the republic of Geneva did in Calvin's time—or otherwise persecuted them in a manner repulsive to our moral standards—colonial Massachusetts may serve as an example. . . .

Now for our experiment. Let us transport ourselves into a hypothetical country that, in a democratic way, practices the persecution of Christians, the burning of witches, the slaughtering of Jews. We should certainly not approve of these practices on the ground that they have been decided on according to the rules of democratic procedure.[2]

Schumpeter's conclusion is that "there are ultimate ideals and interests which the most ardent democrat will put above democracy." "Democracy," he argues, "is a political method." Although it has instrumental value, it is "incapable of being an end in itself, irrespective of what decisions it will produce under given historical conditions."[3]

His point is that if such persecutions were passed by democratic procedures, the mere fact that they were passed in that way would not legitimate them. We would have to overrule the procedural principle in order to condemn them. As an ultimate ethical criterion ("end in itself"), democracy has this theoretical defect.

In our definition of tyranny, the imposition of these severe deprivations on a losing coalition defines the tyrannous alternative. Furthermore, not imposing such deprivations defines an alternative that, by itself, imposes no severe deprivations on anyone. For no matter how strongly the winning coalition may feel about the imposition of such deprivations, that preference is a public-regarding, and not a private-regarding, one. Hence its denial cannot constitute a severe deprivation. Of course the argument need not be confined to the extreme persecution of religious sects. The argument can be generalized to any severe deprivation imposed, in a procedurally correct manner, on any losing coalition.

The vulnerability of all purely procedural principles, other than those requiring unanimity, is that all such principles would legitimate the adoption of a policy imposing any such deprivations—provided only that it has support from those specified by the decision rule. Any procedural principle would *require* that the deprivation be imposed as long as it had the specified support. This consequence follows from the fact that procedural principles were defined as those that would legitimate any action of a regime decided on in the required manner.

Now it will be useful to distinguish two ways in which the imposition of such deprivations may be brought about. They may result from the adoption of a new policy or from the failure to adopt a new policy; they may result, in other words, from a regime's commissions or from its omissions.

More precisely, by a *commission,* I mean a *change* in policy, and by an *omission,* I mean a *continuation* of existing policies. Hence some "commissions" will actually be changes in policy that produce a failure to act, for example, a cancellation of programs previously adopted, while some "omissions" will actually be retentions of policies that produce a continuation of action, for example, the noncancellation of programs previously adopted. Hence objections to policy omission include objections to the nonenactment of new policies as well as to the continuation of old ones; objections to policy commission include objections to the enactment of new policies as well as to the cancellation of old ones.

The status quo has no privileged position in this analysis, although retention of the status quo should never be left out if it is a possible policy. It should be emphasized that retaining the status quo can involve severe deprivations through policy omission just as changes in policy may involve severe deprivations through policy commission. For example, if X will starve or suffer severe consequences if his share of food or medical resources is not increased, the maintenance of the status quo distribution can impose a severe deprivation upon him. If severe deprivations brought about by both omissions and commissions are taken into account, no decision rule is immune from the legitimation of simple tyranny.

Dealing with commissions first, it should be obvious that any non-unanimous decision rule can impose severe deprivations—by commission —on the subset of its members whose support is not required for adoption of a new policy. Depending on the precise decision rule, this losing coalition can be at least equal to one and must be less than the total number of members (a nonunamimous decision rule can require support from any proportion or group of members who number less than the total and at least one).

With regard to possible decision rules, it is true that as the number required for approval of a new policy approaches unanimity, the maximum size of a coalition that can unsuccessfully oppose a new policy shrinks to zero. If unanimity is the decision rule, then, by definition, a new policy cannot be adopted if it is opposed even by one member. Does this mean that unanimous decision rules cannot impose tyranny?

We must distinguish groups that lose by policy commission from groups that lose by policy omission. For once severe deprivations resulting from *omissions* are taken into account, then even unanimity can impose tyrannous choices on a large portion of the population. It is true that under unanimity even one person can always avoid losing by policy commission. But, of course, *everyone* except one person can, therefore, lose by policy omission. Anyone has a veto. Anyone can, by himself, produce a policy omission that affects everyone else.

How may deprivations be imposed by omission? Imagine only that some group requires food to avoid starvation (perhaps there has been a famine) or some group requires emergency assistance or medical care (perhaps there has been a flood or other natural disaster) and that such events pose a new policy problem. If there is not an already existing policy, the veto of any new policy could have consequences as dreadful (for all of those apart from the blocking coalition) as any acts of commission discussed above. Or, suppose the issue is not a new one but merely an old one about which agreement has never been reached. Perhaps there is mass poverty and a small wealthy elite who are just sufficiently numerous to block any redistribution. The continuing absence of any redistributive measures (unemployment compensation, medical care, food assistance) could deny the satisfaction of basic human needs to the bulk of the population.

Once omissions are taken into account, it should be obvious that unanimity is no more successful than any other decision rule in preventing a regime from imposing (avoidable) severe deprivations. In particular, the claims made for the unanimity rule by such writers as Robert Paul Wolff and Buchanan and Tullock appear preposterous in this light. Wolff, for example, claims that "unanimous direct democracy" would offer "a genuine solution to the problem of authority and autonomy."[4] "The autonomous man, insofar as he is autonomous, is not subject to the will of another."[5] Unanimous direct democracy is offered to us as the only state that always preserves individual "autonomy" in this sense. Wolff reasons that "under unanimous direct democracy, every member of the society wills freely every law which is actually passed. Hence, he is only confronted as a citizen with laws to which he has consented."[6]

If the citizen can suffer as much from the government's failures to act as from its actions, then the unanimity rule will not, of course, prevent him from being "subject to the will of another" with respect to such omissions.[7] The government's failure to act may subject him to the will of others —through the government or through third parties whose actions the government fails to prevent. Not only may such cases violate the "autonomy" of losing coalitions, but they may also subject the losers to severe deprivations imposed tyrannously.

The similarly extravagant claim for unanimity offered by Buchanan and Tullock suffers from the same difficulty. They claim that "when unanimous agreement is dictated by the decision-making rule, the expected costs on the individual must be zero since he will not willingly allow others to impose external costs on him when he can effectively prevent this from happening."[8] If this claim is restricted to commissions, then it is, of course, correct. But once the costs of government inaction (omissions or failures to reach agreement on new policies) are taken into account, there is no reason for an individual to expect his "external costs" to be zero under unanimity.[9]

Once omissions are taken into account, it should be obvious that unanimity is no more successful than any other decision rule in preventing a regime from imposing severe deprivations. Severe deprivations that a regime fails to prevent can be as terrible as those that it decides to impose.

In my discussion of unanimity thus far, I have assumed that if no agreement is reached, existing policies (previously agreed to) continue to be in effect. In terms of the regime's policies, the status quo constitutes the point of no agreement. The unanimity rule has also sometimes been interpreted to imply that if no agreement is reached the government simply ceases to exist.[10] On this interpretation, anarchy constitutes the no-agreement point. But, of course, there is no reason to suppose that the choice of anarchy (that is, a situation where there is no longer a state) will not have worse consequences than the continuation of the status quo (that is, the continuing governance of the regime without the new policy about which there was disagreement). Individuals who will suffer from the government failing to intervene when unanimous agreement is not reached may suffer in the same way under anarchy (since there is then no government to intervene). They are, furthermore, rendered subject to the consequences of a host of other cessations of policy—the lack of police protection, fire protection, and whatever other essential services the state may have provided before its dissolution. It should be evident that this alternative interpretation of the unanimity rule will not save it from its vulnerability to the legitimation of simple tyranny.

The argument encounters an additional complication if the decision rule specified by the procedural principle applies at the level of constitutional choice rather than at the level of policy choice. Suppose there is, for example, unanimous consent to a particular constitution. Should not individuals, if they have actually and explicitly consented to such an arrangement, be bound by whatever results from it?

While it might be granted that there is a *prima facie* case for X's being obligated because he (and perhaps everyone else) actually consented to a constitutional arrangement,[11] would not this obligation be overrideable depending on the content of later actions and decisions by the regime? Consider Hanna Pitkin's example of the minor official in Nazi Germany who continues to carry out his oath of office. Is his explicit consent to the regime enough to obligate him regardless of what policies it later implements? She argues: "Sometimes past promises and oaths are not enough to determine present obligations. Sometimes a man who cites even express oath to obedience, is being not admirable but hypocritical, refusing to recognize where his real duty lies." "While we would not want to say that past oaths and promises count for nothing," she adds, "they cannot be allowed to settle the question."[12]

But the distinctive feature of all procedural principles (universal consent included) is that reference to the procedure would, by definition, settle the question. If the decision rule conferring legitimacy is universal consent to the regime, then that decision rule must settle the question of one's obligations to it, regardless of what the regime's later policies turn out to be (the decision rule defines the necessary and sufficient conditions for legitimate actions by the regime). If the regime changes in conformity with the constitutional arrangement or if the constitutional arrangement itself changes in accordance with the stated procedural principle, the result must be legitimate—because it corresponds to agreements reached under the decision rule. Hence if the constitution were changed so as to deny basic rights to certain groups—as long as the stated constitutional procedures were satisfied—the result would be legitimated. Thus it should be obvious that the strategy of locating the decision rule at the level of constitutional choice does not obviate the possibility that regimes legitimated by the procedure will act tyrannously.

Thus it should be evident that, for both unanimous and nonunanimous decision rules, all procedural principles—all principles that would legitimate *any* action of a regime provided it has the support specified by the stated decision rule—can sanction the imposition by the regime of severe deprivations on some losing coalition. The imposition of such deprivations (via commission or omission) can be *required* by such principles—even when the alternative is a state of affairs that involves no severe deprivations whatsoever.

The implications of Schumpeter's "mental experiment" are thus not limited to majority rule (and other procedural interpretations of democracy). For we may substitute *any* (nonunanimous) procedural principle for the "reader's criteria of democracy" in his argument and reach the same conclusions with respect to commissions (new policies). Furthermore, once deprivations resulting from omissions are taken into account, the argument applies to unanimous procedural principles as well.[13]

Whether they are nonunanimous or unanimous, whether they are for policy choice or for constitutional choice, all procedural principles can legitimate a policy of severe deprivations to losing coalitions. And they would do this when the alternative is a policy of severe deprivations to no one. As ultimate criteria, this is their decisive defect.

9. Absolute Rights Theories

As noted in chapter 1, an absolute rights principle is one that evaluates policies according to whether they conform to the injunction: Never violate the rights of anyone. Following this injunction is taken to be necessary and sufficient for a policy's legitimacy; violation of this injunction is, therefore, sufficient for its illegitimacy. By a *right* I mean an unconditional guarantee that person A will not experience certain consequences (specified by the theory) as the result of the actions of others (or as the result of certain kinds of actions).[1] If, in ways specified by the theory, other persons harm him or interfere with his actions, then they violate his rights.

For an absolute rights theory, it is important that the guarantee be defined in an *unconditional* way. By this I mean that A's claim to be protected from certain consequences (as the result of the actions of others) cannot be dependent upon the enforceability of protection for anyone else. A right cannot be absolute if it is defined so that person A is not protected in a given situation merely because someone else cannot also be protected. So if A has a right (of the absolute kind) to be protected from consequences of type X, he has a right not to have X imposed on him—even if protecting A from X means that someone else (say B) will have X imposed on *him*. In other words, we should be able to determine, in any particular case, whether A has a right not to experience consequences of type X (as a result of the actions of others) without our also having to know whether protecting A requires our not protecting someone else. Absolute rights offer protection regardless of considerations pertaining to the protection of others.[2] In this way they are unconditional.

There is an appeal in absolute rights theories that derives from the extreme simplicity of the basic notion, the injunction: (1) Never violate the rights of anyone. But this apparent simplicity masks two difficulties that will concern us. For, depending upon the precise formulation, all absolute rights theories will either produce logically contradictory results or they will legitimate tyranny. Hence my argument is that those absolute rights theories that maintain logical consistency are also vulnerable to tyrannous counterexample.

Let us divide formulations of the basic absolute rights injunction (1 above) into those that are (a) complete or (b) incomplete in the protection they offer against the imposition of severe deprivations. In other words, a rights theory of the first kind might be defined so that it offers protection against all of those consequences (connected to government action or inaction) that we have defined as severe deprivations. The implications of such an absolute rights theory offering *complete* protection could be summarized as: (2) Never impose severe deprivations. Recall that if one person imposes a severe deprivation on another and the government fails to act to prevent it, then that counts as a severe deprivation imposed by the government, because of its connection to the government's failure to act.

All other absolute rights theories (those whose implications do not correspond to [2]) can be classified as *incomplete* in the protection they offer against severe deprivations. In such cases there are severe deprivations that the government may impose without violating any rights in the sense of rights defined by such theories.

My argument is that complete formulations must be subject to inconsistency, while incomplete formulations must be subject to tyrannous counterexample. The latter formulations are subject to counterexample because they are indifferent between a policy that imposes severe deprivations and a policy that imposes no severe deprivations on anyone.

Consider any complete formulation of absolute rights. Any such formulation will result in inconsistency for any problem in which every alternative open to the regime violates someone's rights. The absolute rights injunction, recall, was *"Never* violate the rights of anyone." One case of rights violations contravenes this injunction as much as numerous cases would. Any principle that minimized the total of rights violations (by violating some rights in order to avoid even greater violations) would fail this requirement. Rather than produce an absolute rights theory, such an attempt would produce the kind of theory Nozick labels—and rejects—as a "utilitarianism of rights."[3]

There are cases in which any complete absolute rights theory will produce inconsistent results. We have only to consider the general case in which, corresponding to each alternative policy A_1, A_2, ... A_n, there is a group of one or more persons G_1, G_2, ... G_n who will suffer severe deprivations under that policy. For this to be possible, *every* alternative (including the alternative of inaction) must be included within this list of alternatives, and for each alternative A_i there must be a corresponding group of persons G_i who will suffer severe deprivations. Hence for every alternative, there is a group whose rights will be violated. This follows from the notion of a rights theory offering *complete* protection from severe deprivations.

Given the enormous variety of consequences that can count as severe deprivations connected to government omissions and commissions, there is no shortage of such cases. It may be useful, however, to dramatize the issue with some brief examples. However, because of the complexities of policy choice, any short discussion that purports to cover all of the (reasonably foreseeable) alternatives must appear crudely oversimplified. With this admission in mind, let us explore two cases that exemplify the problem, even though our brief discussion will surely not do justice to the complexities that would actually accompany either of these situations.

Consider this example suggested by a recent American court case.[4] Imagine a town whose entire economy is based on a single industry that, it is discovered, spews dangerous chemicals into the surrounding air and water. The extreme risk to the health of the surrounding communities becomes demonstrable. But the enormous investment required to eliminate the hazardous pollutants would not be economical for the old plant. The company, if required to cease polluting, would have to shut down.

Let us make the following assumptions:

1. *If the company ceases operations, severe deprivations to some inhabitants of the town are unavoidable. For the end of the plant means, effectively, the end of the town and a way of life for thousands of persons. While some may be only mildly affected, the severe deprivation to the ongoing life plans of others and to the developing life plans of their children could not be completely avoided without massive government investment.*

2. *The government could only make the kind of massive investments that would fully ameliorate all of the severe deprivations if it ceased some other activity—whose cessation would also produce severe deprivations. Similar results would follow from the government directly investing in the expensive antipollution systems that would be required.[5]*

3. *Were the plant to continue spewing forth the dangerous chemicals, the effect on the public health of the surrounding communities would make severe deprivations reasonably foreseeable (not only for residents of the town, but for those of other nearby communities, as well).*

In this example every alternative policy available to the government imposes severe deprivations on someone. An absolute rights theory formulated so as to rule out *any* policy choice imposing severe deprivations would simply produce inconsistent injunctions here, for it would rule out each of the hypothesized possibilities.

Now consider a second example, one further removed from contemporary experience. While it might be argued that this case (unlike the last one) falls outside of ideal theory,[6] it is worth discussing for the clarity with which it illustrates the blind-alley problem.

Imagine a medieval city that attempts to deal with the plague by setting up a kind of quarantine. Every house whose inhabitants show signs of the disease is walled up. These houses are sealed off completely so that nothing can escape. As a result the occupants all die terrible deaths of starvation (or perhaps suffocation). But the policy saves the bulk of the town. A large proportion of the inhabitants, who would surely have perished otherwise, are saved.

Given the existing state of medical knowledge, let us assume that this was the only strategy available that offered reasonable prospects of saving a large portion of the population. (Perhaps there is reason to be confident about the results because it has been tried either in another city or at another time.) Not knowing anything about how the disease is transmitted, only such an extreme measure, with its terrible cost, could be presumed to be effective.

Let us assume then that the available policy alternatives can be distinguished as:

1. *letting the disease run its course (or adopting only remedies known to be ineffectual); or*
2. *the "quarantine."*

It should be noted that the second option can be presumed to impose severe deprivations on some persons who might not otherwise die from the disease, in that a house would have to be quarantined if there were signs of the plague among *some* of its occupants. The paltry state of knowledge about who has the disease or about how it is spread has cruel consequences here.

It should be evident that if (1) and (2) are the only two alternatives, then they *both* impose severe deprivations. Any government that attempted to live up to the injunction "never impose severe deprivations" would find itself in a blind alley.

If every alternative (every possible action or inaction) violates someone's rights, then the absolute rights injunction leads to the prohibition of *every* alternative. But to say of each alternative that it is wrong is to say that it would be right to adopt some *other* alternative (or combination of alternatives) instead.[7] However, every other alternative is also wrong in this kind of case. Hence this self-contradictory set of prescriptions—a moral "blind alley"—results from any complete absolute rights formulation applied to such cases.

The difficulty arises not because all absolute rights violations are classified as bad, but because they are all classified as wrong. For an action to be judged wrong, without qualification, is for it to fall under a strong prescription that it not be done.[8] Suppose there are N alternatives $(A_1, A_2, \ldots A_N)$. I assume that to say A_1 should not be done is to say that some alternative, A_2 or A_3 or . . . A_N should be done instead. But this prescription "do A_2 or A_3 or A_N" is contradicted by the fact that *all* of these alternatives $A_2, A_3, \ldots A_N$ are also classified as wrong (requiring the prohibition "do *not* do A_2 or A_3 or . . . A_N").[9] Hence the inconsistency.

Now this kind of blind alley may be avoided by an incomplete rather than a complete formulation of absolute rights.[10] It is possible, by omitting some severe deprivations from the protection afforded by absolute rights, to rule out such inconsistent injunctions.

Nozick, for example, deals explicitly with the problem in this way. He protects against all actual "boundary crossings" (committed without consent) by proposing a "side constraint" notion of rights. However, objectionable consequences that do not involve such boundary crossings (that is, that do not violate side constraints) are not prohibited in any way by the theory.

His "side constraint" notion provides an absolute rights theory of political legitimacy. Rights are placed "as side constraints upon the actions to be done: don't violate constraints C."[11] The unique legitimacy claimed for his proposed "minimal state" is that it can conform to the requirements of this injunction.

But it can conform to this injunction only because certain actions connected to the violation of rights (particularly failures to act) are not counted as violating rights. His position "will be a consistent one," we are told, if his "conception of rights holds that your being *forced* to contribute to another's welfare violates your rights, whereas someone else's not providing you with things you need greatly does not *itself* violate your rights, even though it avoids making it more difficult for someone else to violate them."[12]

The way in which there is no condemnation for *failures* to help others in Nozick's theory can be seen from the case of "a medical researcher who synthesizes a new substance that effectively treats a certain disease and who refuses to sell except on his terms." His right to refuse to sell the lifesaving drug is legitimated, according to Nozick, by his property rights in it. This researcher's actions, Nozick concludes, do not violate the Lockean proviso about the acquisition of property. They do not make people worse off in a way that would violate their rights. He provides no grounds, in fact, for construing the researcher's actions as a rights violation or as a boundary crossing.[13]

These are instances of a general conclusion of Nozick's theory, highlighted in the preface, that "the state may not use its coercive apparatus for the purpose of getting some citizens to aid others."[14] To do so would be a violation of the rights of those forced to help. On the other hand, *failing* to help is not in itself construed as a rights violation.

Nozick admits that many will find this position objectionable: "They don't *want* to believe anything so apparently callous toward the needs and suffering of others."[15] It is, in fact, precisely these examples—whose apparent "callousness" he admits—that provide us with grounds for our objections.

For his notion of absolute rights avoids the inconsistency problem noted above by defining one option—the failure to act in the sense of refraining from crossing anyone else's "boundaries"—as an alternative that can never, by itself, violate rights.[16] But even though such inactions cannot violate rights in Nozick's sense, they can cause severe deprivations (as we have already seen in our discussion of unanimity). And because these severe deprivations do not violate rights, Nozick's theory must be entirely indifferent to them. It is in this way that his theory becomes vulnerable to tyrannous counterexample.

Before I make a general argument, I want to consider another absolute rights theory that depends, for its consistency, on selectivity in the actions that are prohibited. Nagel offers such an "absolutist" theory:

It is important to specify as clearly as possible the kind of theory to which absolutist prohibitions can apply. We must take seriously the proviso that they concern what we deliberately do to people. There could not, for example, without incoherence, be an absolute prohibition against *bringing about* the death of an innocent person. For one may find oneself in a situation in which, no matter what one does, some innocent people will die as a result.[17]

Such a prohibition would result in incoherence because, on such a theory, "nothing one could do would be morally permissible."[18]

Nagel claims to avoid this problem by his prohibition, not of all actions that *produce* certain results, but rather, of all actions that deliberately aim at certain results.[19] Hence, if you produce bad consequences but do not *intend* to do so, your actions may not be wrong on this view; you may not have violated rights.[20] Both Nagel and Nozick have avoided the first horn of our dilemma by this strategy of being selective in the protection afforded by their absolute rights. They can avoid inconsistent blind alleys if this selectivity removes the absolute prohibition from some alternatives—so that a nonprohibited alternative is always available.

However, it is this very strategy of selectivity that renders absolute rights doctrines vulnerable to tyrannous counterexample. For this selectivity renders them entirely insensitive to the imposition of severe deprivations not protected against by the absolute rights. If a severe deprivation is not ruled out absolutely, it is a matter of utter indifference for such theories. They provide no mechanism, apart from the absolute prohibition, for taking account of such deprivations.

Consider the case in which the bringing about of severe deprivations is not covered by absolute rights. The deprivations might not be covered because they would be brought about by a failure to act rather than an action. Perhaps if food is not provided, people will starve, or if medical care is not provided, people will die of disease. On Nozick's strategy of selectivity, such severe deprivations resulting from failures to act would not count as violations of rights. Or, perhaps the severe deprivations do not count as rights violations because they are not deliberately intended. On Nagel's proposal, such severe deprivations, which result as an unintended by-product of other policy aims, cannot violate rights.[21]

Consider any such policy (A_1) that imposes severe deprivations that are not covered by the absolute rights prohibitions. Because these deprivations do not violate rights, an absolute rights theory must be entirely indifferent to them. For within an absolute rights theory there is only room for two judgments: either a policy is prohibited (because it violates rights), or it is not prohibited (because it does not violate rights). If a policy (A_1) imposing severe deprivations falls into the latter category because it violates none of the proposed rights, then it must be considered to be as good as any other policy that violates no rights.[22]

Now consider such an alternative policy (A_2) that violates no rights—and also imposes no severe deprivations. Perhaps A_2 is the policy of organizing a voluntary project to provide the food or medical assistance denied by A_1. Or perhaps A_2 involves a government project to provide the assistance.[23]

Any absolute rights theory must be entirely *indifferent* between a policy (A_2) that imposes no severe deprivations on anyone and a policy (A_1) of the kind just described, which does impose severe deprivations—but *not* by actions covered by the absolute rights prohibitions. For if neither A_1 nor A_2 violates rights, then they must *both* be equally legitimate policies. The only value posited is nonviolation of absolute rights, and both policies satisfy it equally.

It is in this way that absolute rights theories that avoid inconsistency by removing some deprivations entirely from any prohibition by absolute rights must also become vulnerable to tyrannous counterexample. For by ignoring entirely the imposition of such deprivations, such theories must be indifferent between (that is, they must rate as equally good[24]) an alternative (A_1) that imposes such deprivations as an alternative (A_2) that does not.

It is the very simplicity of such theories—a simplicity that results from their utter dependence on a single injunction—that renders them too clumsy and insensitive for complex cases involving conflicting claims, conflicting rights, or conflicting efforts to avoid severe deprivations.

There might appear, however, to be a way out of this dilemma for absolute rights theories. Our argument has been that absolute rights theories that offer complete protection from severe deprivations produce logically inconsistent results, while absolute rights theories that offer incomplete protection must be vulnerable to tyrannous counterexample. Suppose, however, that an absolute rights theory was formulated so as to offer complete protection, not against all severe deprivations, but only against *tyrannous* severe deprivations.

It is true that such an effort might avoid both of the difficulties presented here. First, if such a theory only protected against tyrannous deprivations, then it could not produce inconsistent results. For tyranny has been defined so that it only obtains when a consistent injunction (to avoid it) is possible. Remember that when every alternative imposes severe deprivations, then *no* alternative is tyrannous. Second, such a theory, by definition, could not legitimate tyrannous choices. For it is precisely those choices (and perhaps only those choices) that such a theory would have been designed to rule out.

However, such a theory does not provide a way out of our critique of absolute rights principles. For such a theory would not qualify, in the first place, as an absolute rights formulation. Remember that for a theory to qualify as an absolute rights theory, it must offer an *unconditional* guarantee. This means that A's protection from consequences of type X stipulated by the theory (for example, severe deprivations) cannot be dependent upon the enforceability of anyone else's protection. This provision is, of course, violated by our definition of tyranny. For according to that definition, A's claim to be protected from severe deprivations is dependent upon whether or not others can similarly be protected. In order to know whether A has a claim to be protected, we require not only a description of the consequences but also a description of whether, when A is protected from severe deprivations, others can be protected, as well. The guarantee offered by the principle of nontyranny is not an unconditional one. The protection against the specified consequences (severe deprivations) is dependent upon whether or not they are tyrannous. But we can only determine if they are tyrannous by examining the alternatives available and concluding whether protecting one person means not protecting another. Hence the guarantee is not unconditional.

If the notion of protection against tyranny is formulated as a right, it is not an absolute right. While nontyranny avoids the apparent simplicity of an absolute rights theory, it also avoids the two difficulties discussed here: first, that absolute rights theories offering complete protection produce inconsistent injunctions, and second, that absolute rights theories offering only incomplete protection legitimate tyranny.

10. Structural Principles

Consider these familiar principles: choose the more equal situation; choose the situation serving the general social welfare; choose the situation best for those at the bottom. According to each of these principles, there is something that has value—welfare, money, satisfaction, perhaps even rights or liberty. How that "something" is parcelled out determines the choices prescribed by such principles.[1]

Let me characterize this group of principles more precisely. As noted in chapter 1, a structural principle is one that will determine any state of affairs, X, to be better, equal, or worse than any other state of affairs, Y, based entirely on the information available from an account of payoffs to positions under X and under Y. By *payoffs* I mean goods[2] or welfare in a sense specified by the principle; by *positions* I mean groupings of individuals, each group consisting of 1/nth of the population listed in order of their shares of goods or welfare. A simple example of such a table of payoffs to positions was presented in table 1.1.

Rawlsian maximin justice (his "general conception") is a structural principle in this sense, for it will prescribe a choice of X or Y based on whichever has the *highest minimum* share of primary goods. If Rawls's "special conception" of justice is, as he believes, a special case of the general maximin notion, then that principle also falls within this critique (for more on this issue, see chapters 12 and 13). If, on the other hand, the special conception evades the argument, it would only do so by offering a different kind of principle—one that was not *structural* in the sense defined here. To the extent that Rawls has actually offered us the kind of theory that he himself believes he is proposing (one compatible with a general maximin distribution of primary goods), then his theory is vulnerable to the general argument of this chapter. Classical and average utilitarianism are also structural principles, for they will prescribe X or Y based on the total or the average welfare under the two situations (information easily calculated from payoffs to positions). A principle of equality (in welfare or in goods) would similarly be structural, since the more equal of two distributions can be calculated from a listing of payoffs to positions.

Another interesting structural principle has been proposed by Douglas Rae. Rae argues that while some principles have the defect that they violate equality and while other principles have the defect that they violate utilitarianism, no acceptable principle should have the defect that it violates *both* equality and utilitarianism at the same time.

While Rawls's maximin principle fails this test, Rae has proposed an alternative that passes it. It has two clauses: (a) For any two alternatives, if one would advantage some stratum of society and disadvantage none, choose that; (b) If no alternative satisfies (a), then choose the more equal one.[3] It should be obvious that any alternative that satisfies (a) must also be preferred on utilitarian grounds (for if some payoffs are increased and none decreased, the total must have increased). Similarly, it is true by definition that any alternative satisfying (b) enhances equality. Hence any choice sanctioned by Rae's principle must either agree with equality or with utilitarianism (or with both).[4] Hence Rae's principle passes his minimum test because it can never violate both equality and utilitarianism at the same time.

I mention Rae's proposal only because it is a new structural principle of exceptional interest. However, like all structural principles, it shares the defect that it would legitimate simple tyranny. Like all structural principles it is subject to the argument I present below.

It is important, in order for a principle to be structural, that the positions be identified *anonymously* in terms of a ranking of goods or welfare; it is not particular individuals whose payoffs are compared under X and Y, but, rather, ranked positions. Structural principles say nothing, in other words, about how particular persons match up to positions under X as compared to how they match up under Y. As long as the structure of the distribution (as judged by payoffs to positions) is improved, principles of this kind will prefer a distribution—regardless of how persons are moved around from one position to another in order to achieve the prescribed structure. A requirement for this kind of anonymity is that payoffs be specified in a way that is *temporally independent.* To know that persons at a given position have certain payoffs at time T_1 is not to know anything, in theory, about what payoffs those persons had (or will have) at any other time T_2. The same persons may have high payoffs at one time and low payoffs at another. These seemingly innocent properties of purely structural principles —such as maximin, utilitarianism, equality, and Rae's proposal—render them all defective as ultimate criteria.

Consider situation X in table 10.1. Under that situation we can rank the positions P_1, P_2, etc., to the Nth position P_N. To each position there corresponds a payoff or share represented by S_1, S_2, etc., to S_N. The payoffs determine a ranking of positions from highest (P_1) to lowest (P_N). Corresponding to each position are persons (I_1, I_2, etc., to I_N) who occupy those positions in situation X.

Table 10.1

X			Y		
Positions	*Payoffs*	*Persons*	*Positions*	*Payoffs*	*Persons*
P_1	S_1	I_1	P_1	S_1	I_1
P_2	S_2	I_2	P_2	S_2	I_3
P_3	S_3	I_3	P_3	S_3	I_4
. . .	. . .	. . .	. . .	. . .	. . .
P_{N-1}	S_{N-1}	I_{N-1}	P_{N-1}	S_{N-1}	I_N
P_N	S_N	I_N	P_N	S_N	I_2

Now consider an alternative state of affairs Y. Y is *structurally identical* to X in that the payoffs to positions are precisely the same as in X (P_1 has S_1, P_2 has S_2, etc.). Y differs from X only in that the assignment of persons to positions is different. Under Y, I_2 has been moved from the second highest position to the lowest one, while I_3 has moved up to P_2 and each individual below I_3 has been moved up one position. In other words, I_2 has been moved to the bottom and each individual below I_2 has been moved up one notch.

I will assume in this example that the differences between *adjacent* positions are minimal while the differences between positions that are not adjacent may be substantial. Hence each individual who is moved up only a single position under Y is not significantly benefited. However, I_2, who is moved from P_2 down to P_N, has experienced an extreme change in his position. In moving from X to Y, we have played a kind of musical chairs in the assignment of persons to positions. While no one has gained much by the change, I_2 has lost badly.

Let us apply any structural principle to the problem of choosing between two alternative policies: (a) retention of X as a status quo, and (b) shift to Y from X.

Now the essential point about this example is that *any* structural principle must be *indifferent* between these two alternatives. For a structural principle was defined as a principle that will evaluate any situation X as better than, equal to, or worse than any situation Y, based *entirely* on an account of payoffs to positions under X and Y. Because X and Y are structurally *identical,* any such principle—whether it be equality, utilitarianism, maximin, or something else—must be indifferent between them. For within the limitations imposed, by definition, on structural principles, they are the same case. For example, they have precisely the same degree of equality, the same total, the same minimum. Because there are no structural considerations at issue in the choice between X and Y, they must be rated equal by any structural principle.

But because they are rated equal by any structural principle, such a principle would legitimate the choice of (b) the shift to Y as an alternative rather than (a) the retention of X. It would legitimate such a choice because there would be, by hypothesis, no grounds for a moral objection to the change. One alternative must be fully as good as the other.

But the alternative that is rated equally good (b) would move I_2 from P_2 to P_N. Assuming that this drastic change in his fortunes is of sufficient importance to I_2, this would involve the imposition of a severe deprivation upon him. Furthermore, this is a deprivation that is accompanied by no substantial benefits to anyone else (since the differences between adjacent positions were assumed to be insignificant) and no improvement on structural grounds—no improvement, that is, in the overall degree of equality, the total goods or welfare, the level at the bottom, and so on.

Because *any* structural principle would, by definition, have to be indifferent between these two policies, any structural principle would, in this case, legitimate simple tyranny: the choice of a policy (b) which imposes severe deprivations as opposed to a policy (a) which imposes no severe deprivation on anyone.

It should be added that there is nothing special about this particular example. Innumerable instances could be adduced where structural principles would legitimate simple tyranny because of their unique focus on the payoffs to positions without any sensitivity to the way persons are assigned to those positions. I_2 in this example could as easily be a large group as an individual. Any number of similar examples could obviously be devised where severe deprivations result from changes in *assignment* to structurally identical positions.

This is the special property of structural principles: They are entirely indifferent to such effects on persons independent of effects on positions. Structural principles have no place for the information that we have introduced by the third columns under X and Y, the information that the persons in particular positions under Y are different from the persons in those positions under X. Yet it is persons and not positions who would experience these moves; it is the life history of particular individuals that would be affected, positively or negatively. Ranked positions, by themselves, are only abstractions from those life histories. My point, in other words, is that an account of payoffs to positions under X and Y may mask the imposition of severe deprivations to persons resulting from changes in the way persons are assigned to positions under X and Y. It is these severe deprivations that render all structural principles vulnerable to tyrannous counterexamples.

One should not be misled by this example into believing that the avoidance of tyranny necessarily leads us to ratify the status quo. While I have just employed an example where the only severe deprivations result from changes from the status quo, there are other important cases where maintaining a status quo imposes severe deprivations.

If this possibility is not made explicit a mistaken objection could be directed at the whole analysis. Consider this example and my reply to it: X' is a distributional status quo, Y' is an alternative that would require substantial redistribution. But Y' would also so heavily tax the rich as to destroy their entire way of life. Suppose that these effects are so severe that they satisfy the restrictive conditions we set for severe deprivations in chapter 4. On the other hand, merely maintaining the distributional status quo does not appear to *impose* any severe deprivations. Hence, the argument would go, maintaining X' would be required if tyranny in my sense is to be avoided. For it would appear to be the only nontyrannous alternative. But this result would rationalize the continuation of an unjust distribution that merely continues the poor in their misery and the rich in their luxury.

Table 10.2 makes the objection more specific (the numbers correspond to some index of primary goods to each stratum of society). It is arguable that Y' would represent an improvement if the lowest level under X' (3)

Table 10.2

X'	Y'
30	6
30	6
3	6
3	6
3	6

represents a sufficiently severe level of degradation. But continuation of X' would appear to be required by my notion of tyranny (assuming that the avoidance of tyranny is valued).

But this objection ignores the possibility, emphasized above, that the continuation of a distributional status quo may by itself impose severe deprivations. The continuation of the X' distribution may, over time, make the persons at the bottom (with the meager distribution of only "3" primary goods) even worse off. They may become worse off, despite a constant distributional share, if they are lacking food or medical care or educational opportunities.

Furthermore, if a constant (but meager) distributional share does not make them actually worse off, it may, nevertheless, keep them in a continuing state of deprivation in the sense we discussed in chapter 5. For it may keep them in the "danger zone" where their subsistence needs are constantly in jeopardy. Or it may deny them (and their children) an adequate life chance. It may be impossible in that society for persons growing up in such poverty to realistically aspire to any of the more highly valued positions in the society.

Hence maintaining the X' distribution would, under these conditions, produce severe deprivations for those at the bottom just as redistributing to Y' might produce severe deprivations for those at the top. *Both* X' and Y' would then impose severe deprivations in this example. If these are the only two alternatives, then neither is tyrannous in the sense defined here. For simple tyranny was defined as the choice of a policy imposing severe deprivations when there was an alternative policy that imposed severe deprivations on no one. There is no such alternative in this case.

Nothing we have said so far settles the question of what should be done when *all* of the policies considered impose severe deprivations. Neither alternative would be tyrannous on these assumptions; deciding which alternative is better is not an issue that will be settled here. The point to be emphasized is that, in this case, the avoidance of tyranny would not require the maintenance of the status quo. The maintenance of a status quo may, over time, produce severe deprivations just like those of any other policy.

Now that we have disposed of this objection it may be useful to return to the central issue. The tyrannous counterexample with which we started is general in its application to all structural principles. It results from one of the defining features of such principles: their exclusive concern with the structure of payoffs to positions without consideration for the *assignment* of persons to those positions.

Consider now a second example, which is equally general in its application to all structural principles. This example depends on the notion of adequate life chances specified in chapter 5.

Imagine a society in which those at the bottom (those at P_N in table 10.3) are barred in some way from *ever* attaining any other positions. Perhaps there is a hereditary caste system; or perhaps there is racial or ethnic

Table 10.3

X			Y		
Positions	*Payoffs*	*Persons*	*Positions*	*Payoffs*	*Persons*
P_1	S_1	I_1	P_1	S_1'	I_1
P_2	S_2	I_2	P_2	S_2'	I_2
P_3	S_3	I_3	P_3	S_3'	I_3
. . .	. . .	. . .	. . .	. . .	. . .
P_{N-1}	S_{N-1}	I_{N-1}	P_{N-1}	S_{N-1}'	I_{N-1}
P_N	S_N	I_N	P_N	S_N'	I_N

discrimination and the bottom position is occupied by members of that group; or perhaps the interaction of poverty with cultural and educational opportunities serves in a more complex way to keep the same group at the bottom from generation to generation.

Whatever the precise factors, let us merely assume that the group of individuals at P_N (that is, group I_N) will always be the same group at the bottom. Unless an explicit policy is undertaken to correct it, the probability that they will remain at the bottom is so overwhelming that it would be fair to say that the individuals at P_N, for all practical purposes, had no prospects of reaching any other position.

Now compare a status quo X with an alternative situation Y. Whatever the requirements of a given structural principle, it is possible for that principle to prescribe Y even though Y has the same persons at the bottom as does X. We need only assume that the S′ payoffs under Y compare to the S payoffs under X in such a way that Y will be preferred to X by the structural principle. If this means that the S′ payoffs must have a higher total or be more equal or have a higher minimum—or whatever other *structural* requirement is specified by the principle—let us assume that the payoffs under Y live up to that requirement. However, the bottom group under Y (I_N) is the same as the bottom group under X.

Now let us imagine that over many years, perhaps over many generations, choices that have the characteristics attributed to Y are offered in comparison to status quos such as X. *Any* structural principle will then be committed to a sequence of choices that legitimate group I_N being kept in conditions forever denying them an adequate life chance. In other words, structural principles, because they are defined anonymously, must be insensitive to the question of whether those who start out at the bottom always stay at the bottom.

This result would follow even if, whenever Y was offered as an alternative, there was some other alternative, let us call it Y′, that involved "affirmative action" efforts (perhaps at some cost in efficiency) to the group (I_N) stuck at the bottom. We have only to assume that Y′ is always slightly inferior on structural grounds to Y (perhaps because of the costs of affirmative action).[5] Hence, over a long sequence of choices, the Y′ policies, which would raise the life chances of those at the bottom, would be constantly rejected in favor of the Y policies—policies that continue to bar group I_N from any prospects of rising from the bottom position. For without policies explicitly aimed at raising group I_N from the bottom, the causal factors already operative can be expected to keep them there.

The continuing effects of the caste system (or the discrimination or the complex of cultural and economic conditions) that bars group I_N from ever rising from the bottom constitute a severe deprivation. Hence the maintenance of the system in the face of alternatives offering more adequate life chances (and not severely hurting anyone else) must be simple tyranny. In this, as in the last example, it is the insensitivity of all structural principles to the question of how persons get assigned to positions that renders them vulnerable to tyrannous counterexample.

In the first argument, the severe deprivations resulted from the extreme ways in which persons were moved around; in the second argument, the severe deprivations resulted from the extreme way in which they were *kept* from moving around. In both of these ways, all structural principles —whether their concern is equality or aggregate utility or the share at the bottom (or any other information available from a table of payoffs to positions)—must legitimate tyrannous choices.

In the preceding chapters I have argued that all procedural principles, all absolute rights principles,[6] and all structural principles must be unacceptable as ultimate criteria because they would legitimate tyranny. This argument would not, of course, rule out a role for these principles as weak or *prima facie* criteria—or as considerations that might be brought into play once tyranny has been safely ruled out. However, as ultimate criteria, all of these principles should be rejected because they would legitimate grievous wrongs.

At this point in the essay, a skeptic might object that I have only demonstrated that my principle and all principles of these three kinds must conflict. However, I have not yet demonstrated why my principle should take precedence in these conflicts.

There are two answers to this objection. The first is that the principle that tyranny should be avoided is, I believe, compelling in its own right. It attempts to rule out certain dreadful results when these are entirely avoidable. My method has been to array a class of counterexamples against every principle of a given kind. This is merely a systematic version of a traditional preoccupation in moral theory—the presentation of counterexamples that are thought to be compelling in their own right.

The second answer to this objection is presented in Part Three. For there I argue that, given certain plausible assumptions about rationality and fairness, this principle of nontyranny is the one that would be rationally chosen under fair conditions. There I present a more systematic effort to respond to the question: Why is tyranny so important that it should overrule these other principles?

11. More on Structural Principles: The Compensation Tests and Cost-Benefit Analysis

There is an important subclass of structural principles that merits separate discussion. For these criteria appear, at first glance, not to be structural at all. Furthermore, as the criteria that underlie modern cost-benefit analysis, they have had wide application to policy questions ranging from the construction of dams and highways to the value of life itself.[1] They are now so routinely employed that their adequacy as ethical criteria for social choice should be extensively aired.

I have in mind the tests of hypothetical compensation developed by Kaldor and Hicks and Scitovsky.[2] These tests appear to avoid classification as structural criteria. Because they appear to be defined entirely in terms of *intra*personal choices, they give the appearance of avoiding all interpersonal comparisons (and hence the appearance also of ruling out any account of "payoffs").

Consider a simple two-person case such as the one we discussed in chapter 3. In figure 11.1, U_A is the utility to person A and U_B is the utility to person B. U_A and U_B only require an ordinal representation, so the two axes can be thought of as if they were made of elastic. The irregular lines through points 1 and 2 and through points 3 and 4 are *utility possibility curves*. To adopt the simplest interpretation, they represent the utility to A and B of every possible distribution (between the two persons) of a given quantity of goods. In other words, starting at a given point, say 1, if A started to have some of his goods given to B, A's utility would decrease and B's would increase. If this process were continued, the path of the curve between points 1 and 2 would be traced out. Similar redistributions from B to A, beginning at point 1, would trace out the other end of the curve. The line through points 3 and 4 is the utility possibility curve produced by a larger aggregate quantity of goods.

The compensation tests were offered as a method for arriving at judgments of social welfare in cases falling outside the bounds set by the Pareto principle. As we saw in chapter 3, a utilitarian who took seriously objections to interpersonal comparisons would find himself unable to judge cases where one person was made worse off and another made better off. Starting, for example, at point 1 in figure 11.1, only the points within the quadrant *northeast* of 1 are Pareto-superior to 1. Only such points could be judged better than 1 without interpersonal comparisons. Points outside that quadrant, where one person is made worse off and another better off, are simply noncomparable to 1.[3] There is no way, without interpersonal comparisons, of evaluating whether such points would increase or decrease welfare.

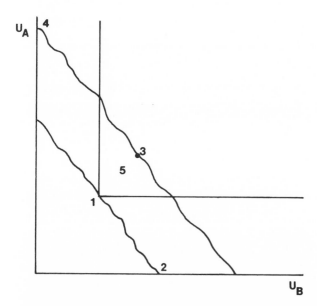

Figure 11.1.

It was in response to this conundrum that Kaldor and Hicks offered the compensation test. As Hicks described it:

How are we to say whether a reorganization of production, which makes A better off but B worse off, marks an improvement in efficiency? The sceptics declare that it is impossible to do so in an objective manner. The satisfactions of one person cannot be added to those of another, so that all we can say is that there is an improvement from the point of view of A, but not from that of B. In fact, there is a simple way of overcoming this defeatism, a perfectly objective test which enables us to discriminate between those reorganizations which improve productive efficiency and those which do not. If A is made so much better off by the change that he could compensate B for his loss, and still have something left over, then the reorganization is an *unequivocal improvement.*[4]

Here is the basic notion of the "perfectly objective test": If there is a change that makes B worse off and A better off, then if A *could* fully compensate B and still be better off after the compensation than he was before the change, the change must be an overall improvement. The central fact is, of course, that this full compensation is hypothetical. If A is advantaged so that he could hypothetically compensate B and still not be worse off, then the change is approved. There is no requirement that this hypothetical compensation actually be carried out. Of course, if it were fully carried out, then B would not have been made worse off at all and the case would then fall within the bounds of the Pareto principle.

In figure 11.1, suppose our status quo is point 1. The question arises, should we move to point 4? Point 4, which would make B worse off and A better off, cannot be evaluated by the Pareto principle. It falls outside of the quadrant northeast of 1 (and also does not enclose point 1 within a northeast quadrant of its own).

But the compensation test would judge point 4 to be preferred to point 1. The reason is that A would have been advantaged so much that he could, hypothetically, move to a point where he could fully compensate B for his losses and *still* be better off than he was at point 1. For the utility possibility curve through point 4 passes to the northeast of point 1. This means that from 4, A and B could move to a point such as 3 where they are both better off than they were at 1. So, according to the compensation test, point 4 should be preferred to point 1 because from 4, A *could* fully compensate B for his worsened situation and still be better off than he was at 1.

There are some aspects of this proposal that need not concern us. There is no need, for example, to discuss the differences between the Kaldor-Hicks version and the Scitovsky version (the difference concerns the contradictory results produced by the former but not the latter, in the event that utility possibility curves cross). For our purposes, we may treat them as a single criterion, for we have no need to discuss the case where utility possibility curves cross.[5]

The four points that we do need to establish are: (a) that the compensation test does not succeed in avoiding interpersonal comparisons, (b) that it does belong in the structural category, (c) that it is vulnerable to the same criticism we have applied to other structural principles, that is, that it would legitimate tyrannous choices, and (d) that even when it is modified by distributional weights (so as to rectify biases resulting from the distribution of income) it would still legitimate tyrannous choices.

Let us examine the first point. The criterion was offered as a "test" for evaluating whether or not a move outside the bounds of the Pareto principle offered a net improvement in social welfare. Hicks reasoned that if A could fully compensate B "and still have something left over," then the result, even without the hypothetical compensation, must be judged an "unequivocal improvement."

But what A would have left over is money (or some equivalent). The inference that such a *potential* Pareto improvement (a point such as 4 from which A *could* fully compensate B) must be an *actual* net improvement in welfare rests on what Baumol has called "a concealed interpersonal comparison on a money basis."[6] As Little argues, it would only hold consistently if this assumption about interpersonal comparisons always applied: ". . . that £1 [or $1] yields the same amount of satisfaction to whomever it is given, rich or poor." Little is not unfair when he adds: "Presumably most people would agree that such an assumption is ridiculous."[7]

However, use of the compensation test as a criterion for social welfare depends on just this assumption. Consider, for a moment, a simple case violating this condition. Suppose that person A gains $200 (or the equivalent) by a change and person B loses $100. This conforms to the assumption that the change is a potential Pareto improvement for A *could* fully compensate B and still be better off by $100. Yet if we could make interpersonal comparisons, it might turn out to be the case that person A gains 2 utils for each dollar he gains and person B loses 5 utils for each dollar he loses. The change has then resulted in an aggregate *loss* in utils because A has gained only 400 utils (200 × 2) while B has lost 500 utils (100 × 5). The change is an aggregate loss in utils even though person A's gain is such that he *could* fully compensate person B and still be better off.

If, however, dollars always produced the same satisfaction for A and B, then it would be impossible for such a case to arise. It would then be impossible for a potential Pareto improvement not to also offer an actual improvement in social welfare. For it would then be the case that whenever A's gain in dollars was sufficient that he could make up for B's losses and have something left over, it must also be the case that A's gain in utility must be sufficient to equal B's losses with something left over. For on this assumption, dollars always produce the same utility for A and B. Under this restrictive assumption, when A's gain more than equals B's loss in dollars, it must also more than equal B's loss in utility.

Hence the compensation test does not avoid interpersonal comparisons. As a criterion for social welfare, it simply is committed to making interpersonal comparisons in one particular—and implausible—way. As Little argued: "It seems improbable that many people would, in England now, be prepared to say that a change which, for instance, made the rich so much richer that they could (but would not) overcompensate the poor, who were made poorer, would necessarily increase the welfare of the community."[8]

So the compensation test can be viewed as *one* version of utilitarianism that incorporates certain dubious assumptions about interpersonal comparisons. It is worth noting, however, that there have been serious efforts to render the assumptions about interpersonal comparisons more realistic. There are versions of cost-benefit analysis that deal with the difficulty just noted through the incorporation of distributional *weights* to compensate for bias resulting from the existing distribution of income. In other words, if we assume that a poor person values an extra dollar more than a rich one, then we can weight dollars to poor people more than dollars to rich ones.[9]

While this strategy responds to the bias noted, it does not save the compensation test from the critique we offer here. For, like all structural principles, the compensation test—with or without distributional weights—can legitimate tyranny.

First, let us deal with the version without distributional weights. Returning to our example in figure 11.1, suppose that we were considering a move from point 1 to point 4. Note that point 4 is the situation where A has *all* the goods and B has nothing whatsoever. Let us assume that if B's share is reduced to nothing (and perhaps maintained there), that must have the effect of a severe deprivation to B. But the compensation test requires that point 4 be preferred to point 1. For, from point 4 we could move along the utility possibility curve to point 3 (which would, hypothetically, more than compensate B for his losses). Hence the compensation test would require that we choose point 4, imposing severe deprivations on B, rather than maintain the situation at 1. Or, similarly, if our choice were between 4 and another point such as 5 (Pareto-inferior to 3), we would be required to choose 4 over 5. In either case, the compensation test requires the choice of an alternative imposing severe deprivations when an alternative (1 or 5) would impose none at all.

But how do compensation tests qualify as structural principles? Recall that we specified in the definition that the payoffs could be listed either in goods or welfare. In the case of the compensation tests, the payoffs are specified in goods rather than welfare. Money, typically, provides a cardinal measure of payoffs.

We can compare any situation to any other if we know the aggregate goods available in the two situations. Consider any status quo X and any alternative to it, Y. If Y involves greater aggregate goods, then any losers under Y *could* be fully compensated—with something left over for the gainers. If, on the other hand, Y does not involve greater aggregate goods, then the move would not be approved. This is the same information traced out for a more complex range of alternatives by the device of a utility possibility curve.

Suppose, however, that distributional weights are incorporated to correct for biases resulting from the existing distribution of income. Then for each alternative policy (or situation) we weight the dollar benefits and losses to each group (so as to take into account the declining marginal utility of money). The result is an estimate of aggregate utility for each alternative. A choice can then be made explicitly on utilitarian grounds. This strategy obviously produces a structural principle where the payoffs are expressed in a measure of welfare resulting from the weightings of dollars to different groups.

The result is, of course, classical utilitarianism. The alternative with the greatest overall utility is chosen. This principle has the same vulnerability to tyrannous choices as any other structural principle. It falls under the general argument presented at the beginning of chapter 10.

Consider two alternatives offering equal aggregate utility: (1) a situation involving equal happiness for everyone, and (2) a situation involving bliss to some and severe deprivations to others. Utilitarians must be *indifferent* between them. There is no moral issue in the choice of (2) rather than (1). Indeed, if (2) produces slightly more aggregate utility, then it must be chosen. It is worth noting that even if distributional weights were incorporated into the calculation of aggregate utility, it would still be possible for a situation such as (2) to be preferred to a situation such as (1). The distributional weights only yield a more accurate *measure* of aggregate utility. If aggregate utility would be served by the imposition of severe deprivations (by the choice of 2), then these would be required by the principle. Here is one last example of a structural principle legitimating tyrannous choices.

Part Three. Justifying Nontyranny

12. Fairness and Nontyranny

Rawls describes the fair way to cut a cake as follows:

Consider the simplest case of fair division. A number of men are to divide a cake: assuming that the fair division is an equal one, which procedure, if any, will give this outcome? Technicalities aside, the obvious solution is to have one man divide the cake and get the last piece, the others being allowed their pick before him. He will divide the cake equally, since in this way he assures for himself the largest share possible.[1]

This method of cutting a cake is offered to us as a model of procedural justice.[2] Because the cake-cutter does not know which piece will be left for him, he must slice them equally if he is to receive the largest share possible. Here rational self-interest is harnessed by conditions of fairness (restricting information) so as to determine a morally appropriate outcome (equality).

It is worth adding that if the situation were altered so that there were "incentive effects" such that making some shares larger would increase the size of the smallest share, then the cake-cutter would choose a *maximin* rather than an equal distribution—for he is only concerned with the size of the last piece.[3]

This cake-cutting procedure is similar, in important ways, to Rawls's famous idea of the original position. In that proposal, rational self-interest is also harnessed by conditions of fairness so as to determine a morally appropriate outcome (maximin).[4] A person is to imagine the principles he would choose, from rational self-interest, if he knew nothing in particular about himself or about his own society. Out of self-interest, he must consider everyone's interests—because he does not know whose interests will turn out to be his own.

The cake-cutting procedure does, however, differ in some essential ways from the method of the original position. The cake-cutter can know particular facts about the cake and how it can be subdivided; the agent in the original position is barred from knowing any particular facts about the society or about how its positions might be arranged (for example, what goods are available to be distributed). Furthermore, the cake-cutter can be sure that if there is a worst piece, it will be left for him; the agent in the original position does not know which position is *already* his. He must decide whether to gamble that it is a desirable one, or whether to play it safe and assume that it is the least desirable one.[5]

The basic idea of the cake-cutter's method is that the person cutting the slices of cake does so in the knowledge that any piece he slights may turn out to be his own. I intend to adapt this notion to policy choice so that the person choosing among alternative policies does so in the knowledge that any position he harms may turn out to be his own.

Of course, like the original position, this proposal is offered as a thought experiment. It is not meant as a method to be institutionalized. Rather, it is a device for clarifying the considerations that justify a principle. As long as it is clear what *would* happen under the appropriate hypothetical conditions, there is no need to actually carry out the experiment.[6] We could, for example, determine that the cake-cutter's method, if applied to an actual cake, would produce an equal division—provided that the choosers acted rationally. We can arrive at this conclusion without any need to experiment on actual baked goods. Furthermore, if faced with an actual problem of dividing a cake, we might regard the principle resulting from the cake-cutter's procedure (under normal conditions this principle would be equality) as having a claim on us—because it defines the results that *would* follow from a fair procedure *if* we were to carry out that procedure. Knowing how equality could be derived as a principle for such cases, we might *invoke* that derivation as a justification for dividing things equally. We could invoke that justification without having to actually reenact the procedure of fair division.

In a similar way, if the cake-cutter's procedure offers a compelling model of fairness for policy choice,[7] then the principle it yields—nontyranny—can be applied without any necessity to reenact the hypothetical procedure that justifies it. My proposal to adapt the cake-cutter's method is thus offered in the same spirit as Rawls's own proposal of the original position. It is a thought experiment to determine the rational choice that *would* be made under the appropriate conditions of fairness.

Suppose we can identify alternative policies A_1, A_2, ... A_N for a given social choice. And suppose we can identify alternative positions P_1, P_2, ... P_N. By positions here I mean identifiable roles or locations within which persons experience the consequences resulting from a given policy. Suppose further that there are individuals I_1, I_2, ... I_N, each of whom will occupy some position under each policy.

I propose the following thought experiment for evaluating the choice among alternative policies: Imagine a rational chooser (say I_1) who chooses among policies A_1, A_2, ... A_N under the hypothesis that everyone else (I_2 ... I_N) *will select their positions under the policy and he will be left with whatever position is remaining.*[8] Just as the cake-cutter designs the slices under the hypothesis that he will have whatever share is left after the others select theirs, our rational chooser selects policies under the hypothesis that he will have *whatever position is left after the others select theirs.*

There are, of course, complexities involved in the notion that a person is to imagine himself in the position of another. For included in the "position" must be whatever preferences of the person (who will actually experience that position under the policy) are crucial to understanding his reaction to the policy. Consider, for example, Sen's problem of distributing beef and pork to devout Hindus and Moslems.[9] Since it would violate their most fundamental convictions for devout Hindus to eat beef, and for devout Moslems to eat pork, the preferences of the persons receiving any particular allotment must be included in the description of how the meat is distributed if we are to evaluate the policy.

In the procedure described above, each alternative policy A_1, A_2, ... A_N would be described by specifying consequences to positions P_1, P_2, ... P_N. The description of these positions must include mention, for example, of whether each recipient of beef or pork under that particular policy is Hindu or Moslem. Hence, the individuals I_1, I_2, ... I_N who are imagined to choose positions must imagine themselves in a position that includes a preference that may be different from their own actual one. This act of imaginatively putting oneself in the position of another, however, is characteristic of universalizable moral reasoning,[10] and is even embodied in the Golden Rule. Hence it is not an unusual requirement for a moral decision procedure.

I wish to argue that, on the basis of a minimal assumption about how these positions are to be evaluated, any rational chooser would select policies according to the principle of nontyranny defined earlier.

I offer only a minimal assumption because of the difficulties facing a more complete basis for choice. What is required for any individual to choose a policy (in the fair decision procedure above) is some theory of interests. He must compare the desirability of different positions under a given policy. This raises, of course, the general dilemma about the evaluation of interests discussed in chapter 3. For this reason I have based my argument on a limited account of interests that appears, within its limited domain, to respond adequately to the general dilemma. For the cases it resolves it would be difficult to argue against it, but it leaves many cases entirely unresolved. It is sufficient, however, to support my proposed principle of nontyranny. Any adequate, more complete account of interests would, I believe, include my minimum assumption.

Suppose that individuals I_1, I_2, . . . I_N are imagined to choose positions according to this minimal assumption: Suffering severe deprivations (as defined in chapters 4 and 5) is worse than not suffering severe deprivations. Our rational chooser would then select a policy that imposed no severe deprivations on anyone as opposed to any policy that imposed severe deprivations on someone. Our chooser (I_1) would select policies in this way because everyone else (I_2, I_3, . . . I_N) would select any nondepriving positions that were available; hence if any positions involved severe deprivations, one of them would be left for him (I_1). The rule of choice that results is equivalent to the principle of nontyranny: Do not choose a policy that imposes severe deprivations when an alternative policy would impose no severe deprivations on anyone; in such cases, of course, choose the nondepriving alternative.

To return for a moment to Sen's problem, suppose there is one distribution of beef and pork that gives beef only to Moslems and pork only to Hindus. Let us call that policy A_1. The other policies (A_2 . . . A_N), let us suppose, all involve some allotments of beef or pork going to persons with the wrong religion (to appreciate that allotment). Let us ignore, furthermore, obvious ways out of the problem by assuming that, for some reason, it is impossible for Hindus and Moslems to trade their shares (perhaps they are physically separated in some way). If the issue is of sufficient importance to them (we might imagine them all on the verge of starvation), any policy other than A_1 would be tyrannous. Furthermore, only policy A_1 would be selected by a rational chooser. For that policy imposes no severe deprivations on anyone. Any other policy would leave our rational chooser, according to the thought experiment, imagining himself in the position either of a starving Hindu stuck with beef or a starving Moslem stuck with pork. Our rational chooser would select A_1—which rules out such severe deprivations for everyone. Hence the rationality (under these hypothetical conditions of fairness) of the principle of nontyranny.

This principle of nontyranny, however, says nothing about cases where *every* alternative would impose severe deprivations on someone. But note that our fair decision procedure would leave those cases similarly indeterminate. For our rational chooser would have no basis for choosing between policies in such a case. By hypothesis, he has only distinguished between positions according to whether or not they involve severe deprivations. If *every* alternative policy would impose a severe deprivation on someone, then the position he would envisage as remaining for him would involve severe deprivations—no matter which policy he chooses.

In this sense, of course, the principle of nontyranny is a radically incomplete principle. It says nothing about many of the most important social choices. For this reason I am arguing for it not as a complete theory, but rather as a minimum condition for acceptable principles. As such a minimum condition it is far from trivial. For as we have seen, *any* procedural principle, *any* absolute rights principle, and *any* structural principle must violate this minimum condition by legitimating tyranny. It is in this sense that this minimum condition has important substantive implications.

How is this derivation of nontyranny to be compared with Rawls's derivation of justice from the original position? In the next chapter I offer a detailed appraisal. For the moment, it is worth noting that both decision procedures share a fundamental conception of fairness.

One formulation of the Golden Rule is: "Do as you would be done by." For the multiperson case this might be generalized to this notion of fairness:

General notion of fairness: *A should decide on a policy affecting B, C, D, etc., only after taking account of how he would wish to be treated were he in the place of B, C, D, etc.*

This is an incomplete definition as long as it lacks specification of how A is to "take account" of his reactions in the place of B, C, D, etc. The original position can be seen as one particular version that completes the definition: the agent in the original position does not know which position is to be his; hence he has to take seriously the possibility that he will turn out to occupy the representative position of any stratum. Rawls then argues that it is rational, because of the special stakes involved, to take with greatest seriousness the possibility of being at the bottom. In the original position an agent ends up making the selection "a person would choose for the design of a society in which his enemy is to assign him his place."[11]

The Rawlsian original position thus offers one version of fairness; my adaptation of the cake-cutter offers another. For a chooser following the cake-cutter's procedure must, if he is rational, consider how he would wish to be treated in any of the positions affected by the choice. For any position he slights may turn out to be the one left for him. Both methods —the original position and the one proposed here—constitute procedural expressions of the general notion of fairness just specified—a notion that makes a deep appeal to reciprocity reminiscent of the Golden Rule.

How these two derivations can be compared is my subject in the next chapter. For the moment I only wish to note that the cake-cutter's analogy is a plausible model of fairness that, when combined with my minimal assumptions about rational self-interest (my account of severe deprivations), yields the criterion of nontyranny. It is in this sense that the principle would be chosen by rational persons under fair conditions.

13. A Critique of the Rawlsian Alternative

In this chapter I compare my argument deriving nontyranny from the cake-cutter's procedure with Rawls's argument deriving maximin from the original position. Rawls's theory is of such importance that I believe any alternative to it—even a partial alternative such as the one I have proposed—must explicitly confront the challenge posed by Rawls's argument. For Rawls claims to have solved the "priority problem."[1] He claims to have arrived at principles that resolve questions of social justice without having to be balanced against other moral considerations. His proposed principles are the ones that should have "priority." Furthermore, he supports these claims with an argument of great force and originality. It is an argument that is too influential and too powerful to be ignored in an essay of this kind.

If I can establish that my derivation for nontyranny should be preferred to his for maximin, then I will have added important, additional support to the criterion of nontyranny. For this reason, a detailed comparison of my proposal with the Rawlsian alternative is warranted at this point.

To compare the derivation offered in the last chapter with Rawls's derivation of maximin from the original position, we must consider two separate sets of issues: first, whether the appropriate account of *fair* conditions for choice is offered by Rawls's account of the original position or by my adaptation of the cake-cutter; second, whether the appropriate account of *rationality* for motivating choice (under those conditions of fairness) is offered by Rawls's account of primary goods or by my account of severe deprivations.

These possibilities can be seen in the simple fourfold table 13.1:

Table 13.1

Rationality	*Fairness*	
	A. Original position	B. Cake-cutter
I. Theory of primary goods	Maximin*	Maximin
II. Theory of severe deprivations	Nontyranny	Nontyranny

My strategy is to establish that the outcomes are those pictured in table 13.1. It should be apparent that if I am correct in identifying these possibilities, then an argument that (II) should be preferred to (I) would be sufficient to establish that nontyranny should be preferred to maximin.[2] For if the appropriate account of rationality (that is, of rational self-interest) is the theory of severe deprivations rather than the theory of primary goods, then nontyranny would be the rational choice—even in Rawls's original position. In other words, the argument that (B) the cake-cutter should be preferred to (A) the original position would not be necessary. I also make the latter argument, however, because I believe that the cake-cutter proposal avoids some serious difficulties to which the original position is subject.[3] Yet it is worth emphasizing that the basic claim turns on the choice between (I) and (II), rather than on the choice between (A) and (B).

Of course this argument only makes the case for nontyranny in comparison to Rawls's argument. However, Rawls has already made a plausible case for the original position in comparison to its clearest rivals.[4] Those alternatives are not discussed here. In this way, my argument depends, admittedly, upon the plausibility of treating Rawls's argument as the major alternative derivation of a social choice principle.

Both Rawls's argument and my own are informal in two ways: first, the list of alternative *decision procedures*—compared to the proposal adopted —is informal; second, the list of alternative *principles*—compared to the proposal adopted—is informal. In each case the list is informal because it does not cover all of the possibilities.[5] We never know, in other words, when someone might come up with an even better proposal.

For these reasons, even if my argument that my derivation of nontyranny should be preferred to Rawls's derivation of maximin were accepted, that would still not secure the argument for nontyranny in a conclusive way. For the list of alternatives with which it is being compared is radically incomplete.

However, I do not aim by this derivation to establish the principle in a conclusive way. Rather, the derivation is meant to dramatize and clarify moral considerations that lie behind the principle. It is meant as additional support for a moral principle that, I believe, is already compelling in its own right.

With these explanations for the status of the argument, let us now turn to the possibilities arrayed in the fourfold table 13.1. Let us begin with (IA). I have placed an asterisk by "maximin" there to indicate that this is the principle that Rawls believes would be chosen under his stated assumptions. However, I will offer grounds for disputing that this is the case.

The argument for maximin from the original position rests on "three chief features" that apply in that situation. The first feature is that "the situation is one in which a knowledge of likelihoods is impossible or at best extremely insecure."[6] "The second feature that suggests the maximin rule," Rawls tells us, is that "the person choosing has a conception of the good [that is, of his interests] such that *he cares very little, if anything, for what he might gain above the minimum stipend that he can, in fact, be sure of by following the maximin rule.* It is not worthwhile for him to take a chance for further advantage, especially when it may turn out that he loses much that is important to him [Emphasis added]."[7] Rawls adds, "This last provision brings in the third feature, namely, that the rejected alternatives have outcomes that one can hardly accept. The situation involves grave risks."[8]

The significance of the first feature is that it undermines the kind of probabilistic calculations that would support the choice of an alternative criterion—average utility. Rawls demonstrates that if one were to calculate probabilities on the basis that when there is no other relevant information, all possibilities are accepted as equally likely (the principle of insufficient reason), then *average utility* would be the rational choice from the original position.[9] This would, however, involve a gamble based on inferences that are only appealing when all reliable information is lacking. Rawls argues that the first feature—that there is no basis for probabilistic calculations apart from the principle of insufficient reason—when combined with the second and third features, makes the risk of such a blind gamble too great.

Since the significance of the first feature is primarily to bar the argument for average utility, let us turn to the second and third features. It is these features that apparently imply maximin.

The second and third features imply that there is some amount of primary goods—an amount that can be guaranteed for everyone by maximin—that has two properties: (a) according to the second feature, we should care little if anything, from the original position, for more than that amount; (b) according to the third feature, less than that amount would be disaster.

Let us call the amount of primary goods corresponding to (a) and (b) (the second and third features) Z. If Z primary goods can be guaranteed by maximin, then, Rawls argues, maximin should be chosen in preference to average utility or any of the other principles he considers. For maximin would rule out the disaster resulting from less than Z. And there is no compelling reason to require more than Z, given the second feature. Because agents in the original position should be satisfied to secure at least Z, they should settle on maximin.

I do not believe that this argument is successful in justifying maximin. Rather, it implies a principle that might be called a guaranteed minimum.[10] For purposes of argument, let us accept Rawls's assumption that, in the original position, it is rational to apply the three features to the evaluation of shares of primary goods. This means that there is some amount of primary goods, which we have called Z, such that more than Z would not be highly valued, and such that less than Z would be disastrous. This means, evidently, that it would be rational for agents in the original position to agree to secure Z for everyone.

But this latter conclusion is quite different from maximin. For maximin requires, not that a particular minimum, Z, be secured for everyone, but that the minimum continue, over time, to rise as far as possible. Imagine a series of principles that share, as a first requirement, that Z primary goods be given to everyone. One principle, however, prefers the more equal distribution—provided that no one has less than Z. Another principle prefers the distribution with the highest totals—provided that no one has less than Z. Another prefers the highest minimum possible—again, maintaining the requirement that no one has less than Z.

Rawls's argument is that the last principle just mentioned must be chosen in the original position. But it is only one of innumerable principles that fully satisfy the assumptions he has posited. For we might devise any number of principles that provide at least Z as a guaranteed minimum for everyone. For example, versions of utilitarianism and equality, when constrained by this requirement, satisfy the argument fully as well as maximin. To claim maximin as the *unique* solution is too strong a conclusion to draw from the stated assumptions. Only the more limited claim of a guaranteed minimum actually follows from those assumptions.

While maximin offers one of many strategies for ensuring a guaranteed minimum, it also has other important implications that are not justified from the assumptions available to agents in the original position. Central among these implications is the prescription that after Z has been secured for everyone, further increases must go, as far as possible, to the minimum position rather than to any other. Rawls's stated assumptions are simply insufficient to settle this question. It is in this sense that maximin is too strong a conclusion to draw from the original position. Maximin does not clearly hold with "priority" in comparison to other possible principles that would also provide Z for everyone. This mistake is discussed further in Appendix B. For now, let us set aside case (IA).

I have already alluded to the argument for maximin in (IB). Given a theory of goods to be distributed—such as Rawlsian primary goods—an agent cutting the cake, that is, allocating goods to positions, would only be concerned to make the worst position as desirable as possible. For, by hypothesis, the worst position is the one that will be left for him.

For these purposes I interpret the "three features" as a requirement of the original position and not of the theory of primary goods itself. For elsewhere Rawls states that agents know that "they want more rather than less primary goods."[11] To derive maximin from the cake-cutter's method we need this assumption that an index of primary goods has been defined such that more is preferred to less by everyone. The rational chooser (cake-cutter) must then maximize the minimum share if he is to maximize his own. For the minimum share is the one that will be left for him.[12]

Therefore, *if* we had a workable theory of primary goods, and if I am correct in my adaptation of the cake-cutter, then maximin would follow from my fair decision procedure. However, we are lacking an adequate theory of primary goods. We lack, in effect, a theory of the "cake" to be subjected to the cake-cutter's procedure. Furthermore, the development of such a theory faces formidable difficulties—as we will see in discussing the (IIA) possibility.

Let us now turn to possibilities (IIA) and (IIB). In other words, what would be chosen in the original position and in the cake-cutter's procedure if the account of rational choice is the one provided by the theory of severe deprivations specified above? Possibility (IIB) has already been worked out in chapter 12. My contention there was that the principle of nontyranny would be chosen in the cake-cutter's procedure if everyone were motivated to avoid severe deprivations.

The remaining possibility is (IIA). What would be chosen in the original position if the account of rational self-interest were provided by the notion of severe deprivations? In dealing with this problem I employ, as far as possible, the same assumptions in the original position as those that Rawls employs. In particular, it is worth noting that he only bars the argument for average utility by assuming the "three features." Without the three features, it is an open question whether average utility or maximin is the more rational choice.

Elsewhere I have argued that the three features are not themselves justified by the other assumptions invoked to support them.[13] For this reason, they do not serve to settle the question of which principle is the more rational choice in the original position.

This problem is twofold. Without the three features, on the one hand, choice in the original position is inconclusive. There are alternative arguments (for radically different conclusions) that appear equally reasonable.[14] With the three features, on the other hand, assumptions crucial to determining the choice appear to be unjustified and perhaps ad hoc. On either account there is no determinate choice that is not easily contestable. These are fundamental difficulties with the argument from the original position—difficulties that are avoided entirely by the alternative procedure proposed here (the cake-cutter). For in that procedure there is no role for the three features. And without the three features, there is a clear result —my proposed principle of nontyranny.

However, in considering what would result in Rawls's original position, we must employ the three features. For without them the vulnerability to utilitarian counterarguments makes the problem of choice indeterminate and hotly contestable. I invoke the three features only to consider the question of what would follow from the original position if my account of severe deprivations were substituted for Rawls's theory of primary goods. However, I believe that the most adequate of these derivations—the one that avoids all of these difficulties involving the three features—is provided by (IIB), that is, my derivation of nontyranny from the cake-cutter's procedure. Hence in the argument that follows I employ the three features without justifying them. But I am doing so for comparative purposes only.

My remedy for the difficulties in the three features is the alternative argument based on the cake-cutter.

It would not, in fact, be implausible to apply the three features to severe deprivations in the original position. In particular, let us assume that suffering severe deprivations must be considered a disaster. Furthermore, let us assume that this disaster is of such importance that it would not be worth gambling on more advantageous results if this meant risking such a disaster. On this account then, an agent is motivated, most of all, to avoid having severe deprivations imposed on him. These assumptions amount to the second and third features.

I believe that, for this reason, if an agent in the original position were asked to formulate a prescription for policy choice (which is clearly a *part* of the problem of justice in the original position[15]), he would agree to rule out the choice of policies imposing severe deprivations when he could choose an alternative policy that would not impose severe deprivations on anyone. For, by the three features, it is not rational for him to gamble on being one of those who does *not* suffer from the severe deprivations (that is, gamble on being someone who benefits when severe deprivations are imposed on someone else). He cannot support a policy that imposes any severe deprivations—when these could be avoided for everyone—because he must take seriously the possibility that *he* will turn out to be among the losers. Under these conditions it is rational for him to choose "as if his enemy is to assign him his place."[16]

Now it is also possible that agents in the original position might choose to add provisions to the principle of nontyranny. In other words, nontyranny, as a criterion, is radically incomplete. There are many important cases that it does not decide. These may be divided into two categories: (a) cases where no alternative policy imposes severe deprivations, and (b) cases where every alternative policy imposes severe deprivations.

I believe that, depending on how the three features are interpreted, an argument can be made that agents in the original position might *add* to the criterion of nontyranny further provisions that decide cases of the (b) kind. In particular, they might be interested in limiting the *number* of severe deprivations when *some* severe deprivations are unavoidable.[17] But whether or not they would add such provisions to the criterion of nontyranny, it should be clear that under these assumptions they could rationally agree on at least that much. At *least* the criterion of nontyranny would be agreed to under (IIA). Whether or not more would be agreed on need not concern us.

We have now examined each of the outcomes in the fourfold table. If I am right in these inferences about what would be chosen in each case, then to establish the priority of nontyranny—compared to Rawls's claim for maximin—I need only establish that (II) should be preferred to (I). For if the account of severe deprivations is accepted as the basis for rational choice, then nontyranny follows from *either* of the two choice procedures —Rawls's original position or my adaptation of the cake-cutter's method.

Hence I only need to argue that the account of severe deprivations should be preferred, as a basis for choice, to Rawls's theory of primary goods. I present two arguments: (1) the doctrine of primary goods as presently formulated makes any substantive solution to the problem of justice impossible,[18] and (2) there are ethical reasons for accepting the priority of the account of severe deprivations whenever that account might support different conclusions than would Rawls's doctrine of primary goods. Obviously, (2) is the argument of most direct relevance to our problem. However, (1) is also of importance, for it undermines the sense in which the two upper possibilities in our fourfold table (the [I] possibilities) offer a real alternative. I begin with this claim that the doctrine of primary goods as presently formulated makes any substantive solution to the problem of justice impossible.

Rawls presents two versions of his principles of justice—the "general" and "special conceptions." The general conception is defined as follows: "All social values—liberty and opportunity, income and wealth, and the bases of self-respect—are to be distributed equally unless an unequal distribution of any, or all, of these values is to everyone's advantage."[19] Obviously, the only way in which an *inequality* could be to *everyone's* advantage (including those at the bottom) is for an increase in inequality to be accompanied by an increase at the bottom. In such a case the bottom sectors would be better off in an unequal society than they would be in a more equal one. This general conception is, as Rawls notes, equivalent to the maximin rule for primary goods, in general.

But to know how to evaluate a share of primary goods, we must have an index—a scheme for comparing heterogeneous shares of "liberty and opportunity, income and wealth, and the bases of self-respect." Rawls's response to this problem is the special conception. This version specifies a serial or "lexical" order for the various primary goods. First, liberty has priority over all other primary goods. Second, fair equality of opportunity is next in lexical order. Last in order is the principle that income and wealth are to be distributed in maximin fashion.[20]

These priority rules are based on claims about the comparative values of the various primary goods: "The serial ordering of principles expresses an underlying preference among primary social goods. When this preference is rational so likewise is the choice of these principles in this order."[21]

Even if we were to grant Rawls the general conception, the choice of an index of primary goods would crucially affect the principle that resulted. Rawls's particular proposal is the comparative rankings embodied in the special conception. However, other possible indexes would lead to quite different principles. Consider, for example, the principles that would result in these cases: (a) if money were ranked above equal opportunity, (b) if equal opportunity were ranked above liberty, or (c) if equal opportunity, liberty, and money were all commensurable so that they could be traded off according to specific weights. Obviously, the general conception (the general maximin notion) could lead us to entirely different principles depending on which index is chosen.

On what basis would Rawls have us choose an index of primary goods? How are we to choose between the very different ways in which shares of primary goods might be evaluated? Rawls's answer is contained in the theory of rational life plans. It is this theory that must provide the grounds for any claim that the index contained in the special conception is to be preferred, in the original position, to possibilities such as (a), (b), and (c) above.

I argue, however, that on his stated assumptions, this problem is insoluble. There is no basis for concluding, in the original position, that one index of primary goods (such as the rankings in the special conception) will further an agent's rational life plan better than other possible indexes, such as (a), (b), or (c). There are many alternative indexes that have an equivalent claim based on these assumptions. And each of these indexes produces a quite different substantive principle of justice. It is for this reason that Rawls's doctrine of primary goods based on rational life plans leaves the problem of justice indeterminate. For it leaves us with no basis for choosing one principle (such as the special conception) over innumerable rivals derived from alternative indexes. For these alternative indexes can, with equal plausibility, claim to advance rational life plans.

Rawls must show that one scheme for evaluating primary goods is appropriate—regardless of an agent's particular rational life plan. For an agent in the original position must make a choice out of self-interest while knowing nothing in particular about himself. Most importantly, he cannot know his particular rational life plan. If, however, he could be sure that *whatever* his rational life plan more primary goods evaluated according to one particular index (rather than another) furthered that plan, then he could arrive at a choice out of self-interest.

Is some index of primary goods to be preferred to its possible alternatives because of its connection to the general notion of rational life plans? If, in the original position, I know merely that I have *some* rational life plan, am I justified in choosing the rankings of the special conception (liberty, then equal opportunity, then income and wealth in serial order) rather than schemes such as (a), (b), or (c) above?

Suppose we were to accept, for purposes of argument, Rawls's proposed account of rational life plans. Does it support, uniquely, the choice of one particular scheme for evaluating primary goods?

Rawls defines rational life plans as follows:

A person's plan of life is rational if, and only if, (1) it is one of the plans that is consistent with the *principles of rational choice* when these are applied to all the relevant features of his situation, and (2) it is that plan among those meeting this condition which would be chosen by him with *full deliberative rationality,* that is, with full awareness of the relevant facts and after a careful consideration of the consequences.[22] [Emphases added.]

Condition (1) is satisfied by any plan consistent with (a) the "principle of effective means," which requires that "means" be efficiently employed toward the fulfillment of "ends"; (b) the "principle of inclusiveness," which requires that the larger set of desired ends be fulfilled in preference to one of its subsets; and (c) the "principle of the greater likelihood," which requires, other things being equal, that the plan more likely to be successful be chosen. These are the "principles of rational choice."[23]

It should be evident that a wide variety of plans requiring a wide variety of conditions for their fulfillment might well satisfy condition (1) defined in this way. Furthermore, condition (2), the requirement that a plan be chosen with full awareness of conditions and consequences, falls far short of resolving the difficulty. Any plan that *anyone* would choose for himself with full awareness in the "deliberative" sense and according to these principles of rational choice may thus qualify as rational. Furthermore, for any given individual, there is not one plan but a "maximal class of plans"[24] that might be reasonably chosen. Only the person himself may decide, in the final analysis, on the particular plan (drawn from the maximal class of plans) that alone determines his good.[25]

In principle, there are few, if any, limits on the variety that plans may assume and still qualify as rational. As Rawls admits, "From the definition alone very little can be said about the content of a rational plan, or the particular activities that comprise it."[26] We are asked, for example, to consider the following case:

Imagine someone whose only pleasure is to count blades of grass in various geometrically shaped areas such as park squares and well-trimmed lawns. He is otherwise intelligent and actually possesses unusual skills, since he manages to survive by solving difficult mathematical problems for a fee. The definition of the good forces us to admit that the good for this man is indeed counting blades of grass, or more accurately, his good is determined by a plan that gives an especially prominent place to this activity.[27]

If the grass-counter's way of life can count as a rational plan, then how are we to justify the rankings in the special conception compared to indexes such as (a), (b), and (c), mentioned earlier? The grass-counter would seem to require few, if any, of these primary goods. What need has he for political liberty or equal opportunity, for example? What need has he for freedom of conscience? Or, for that matter, how demanding is he about wealth or income?

Or, consider the rational life plan of an aspiring capitalist entrepreneur. He might, for example, be benefited greatly by a scheme that allowed sacrifices of liberty for economic development. Such trade-offs are, of course, absolutely ruled out by the rankings in the special conception.

Or consider the member of a minority group whose life plan may require *more* than the share of opportunity Rawls has prescribed. Rawls's notion of fair equal opportunity requires that "those with similar abilities and skills should have similar life chances."[28] By this, Rawls means that "those who are at the same level of talent and ability, and have the same willingness to use them, should have the same prospects of success regardless of their initial place in the social system, that is, irrespective of the income class into which they are born."[29]

The difficulty with this notion of equal opportunity, as Rawls admits, is that "even the willingness to make an effort, to try, and so to be deserving in the ordinary sense is itself dependent upon happy family and social circumstances."[30] Some persons may never have a chance to *develop* the talents and motivations, in the first place, that would qualify them for the benefits of fair equal opportunity. Such cases will arise as long as the institution of the family provides unequal developmental opportunities to some—and fails to provide them for others. Hence some people may

require *more* than equal opportunities. Without more than equal opportunities—which may infringe on the opportunities and liberties of others
—their rational life plans may be destined for failure.

It should be obvious that an agent in the original position cannot be
confident that adoption of the precise rankings in the special conception
will further his own rational plan of life more than that plan would be
furthered by any of the other rankings we have considered. For an agent in
the original position only knows that he has *some* rational plan. Given the
dizzying variety of possible rational plans, his plan might not be furthered,
indeed it might be hindered, by adoption of the special conception rather
than an alternative.

Thus the doctrine of rational life plans does not in itself determine a
choice among the possible schemes for evaluating primary goods. This
means, however, that if the problem of justice requires such a scheme for
its solution, then the problem, within these assumptions, is unresolvable.
For there are innumerable alternative ways of evaluating primary goods
that would further *some* rational plans. And there are no schemes that can
claim to best further *every* plan. Compare the special conception, for
example, with a scheme that placed equal opportunity first and liberty
second. Is there anything in the general doctrine of rational life plans that
might suggest to an agent in the original position that this scheme would
further his life plan worse than would the special conception? There is no
basis for determining a choice between such alternatives in the original
position—even though a principle emphasizing equal opportunity first
would have entirely different substantive implications.

Because the doctrine of rational life plans is compatible with many
different schemes for ranking primary goods, it leaves the problem of
justice indeterminate. For even if we were to grant Rawls the general
conception, for purposes of argument, radically different principles would
follow from alternative indexes that, on these assumptions, have an equivalent basis. It is for this reason that Rawls's notion of primary goods based
on rational life plans does not permit a solution to the problem of justice.
Rather, it leaves it indeterminate.

But these defects in the doctrine of primary goods only undermine the
sense in which that doctrine imples an alternative solution. There are other
reasons of more direct relevance to our problem for preferring the account
of interests offered by severe deprivations.

There is a difficulty in comparing the account of severe deprivations offered here and Rawls's doctrine of primary goods. That difficulty is that Rawls's doctrine amounts to a far more complete theory of interests. The account of severe deprivations makes only a limited discrimination—either a person X suffers a severe deprivation or he does not. In other words, either his essential interests have been destroyed or they have not been. This limited discrimination is sufficient to support the judgments required by the principle of nontyranny (that is, the principle that simple tyranny must be avoided). However, a wide range of choices are left undecided.

Yet if I can establish that my proposal offers the preferred account of interests—for the judgments it does support—then I will have justified the principle of nontyranny. For if a more complete account were to be developed that included the doctrine of severe deprivations—and other judgments besides—this could not affect my argument. For that argument is intended to support *at least* the principle of nontyranny. In other words, if a more complete, but consistently nontyrannous, principle were derived from one of these decision procedures, that would not affect my position. As long as at least nontyranny results, my argument will have succeeded.

There are, of course, cases where the two accounts of interests yield similar conclusions. X may suffer a severe deprivation and, at the same time, a substantial loss in primary goods. However, consider these two cases where the accounts diverge:

1. *X suffers a severe deprivation without a comparable loss in primary goods;*

2. *X suffers a substantial loss in primary goods but no severe deprivation.*

In each of these cases, there is a conflict between the limited discrimination supported by the notion of severe deprivations, on the one hand, and the judgments supported by the theory of primary goods, on the other. My argument is that in both of these cases, my notion of severe deprivations offers a more adequate account of X's essential interests.

In case (1) the doctrine of severe deprivations would tell us that X's essential interests have been destroyed. However, the account of interests offered by Rawlsian primary goods would provide no basis for such a judgment. Which account should take priority?

If X has not suffered a loss in primary goods, then, according to Rawls, X retains certain "means" for the realization of his rational life plan. Liberty, equal opportunity, income, and wealth are valued because—whatever the details of one's rational plan—they are a "necessary means."[31] They are not held to be sufficient, but only necessary. A rational plan may still fail, even with an abundance of primary goods.

Now if X suffers a severe deprivation, then his *actual* personal life plan (in our proposed sense) has, in fact, encountered a decisive defeat. Note that X's actual personal life plan may be quite different from his rational plan of life in Rawls's sense. For the latter, as we have seen, is the one that he *would* rationally choose for himself with full knowledge of conditions and consequences: "A rational plan is one that would be selected if certain conditions were fulfilled. The criterion of the good [that is, the good of an individual—his rational self-interest] is *hypothetical* in a way similar to the criterion of justice [Emphasis added]."[32]

The argument for preferring the account of severe deprivations to the account of primary goods in case (1) is twofold. First, if we know that X has *not* suffered a substantial loss in primary goods, we are only then entitled to conclude that a *necessary* condition for X's rational life plan has been preserved. We cannot conclude that X's rational life plan has avoided defeat. For that plan may fail in many other ways than through a loss of primary goods. In other words, even if we were to accept, for purposes of argument, that the Rawlsian rational life plan provided the basis for judging X's interests, we could not conclude that X's rational life plan was prospering merely from the fact that X retained his primary goods. Primary goods are, at best, only a necessary means.

Second, there is a crucial difference between the plan X *would* choose under conditions of extensive knowledge and clear-headed rationality and the plan he actually lives. Surely the one he actually lives, which defines his ongoing projects, his hopes, and his aspirations, is the one whose defeat would destroy his essential interests. For his *hypothetical* rational life plan in the Rawlsian sense could be rendered impossible and he might never know it. How would it affect him? What essential interest of his would be destroyed if the path blocked were the path *not* taken? If the two accounts of interests diverge, it is when X actually suffers a severe deprivation that we can be most confident that his essential interests have been destroyed.

Now consider case (2). X suffers a substantial loss in primary goods but no severe deprivations. Have X's essential interests been destroyed? Again, there are two reasons for preferring the account offered by severe deprivations. The first concerns the loose connection between primary goods and Rawlsian rational life plans; the second concerns the disparity between X's rational life plan and the plan of life he actually lives.

While primary goods are supposed to constitute a "necessary means" for the fulfillment of rational life plans, Rawls admits that some rational life plans will turn out *not* to require them:

Of course, it may turn out, once the veil of ignorance is removed, that some of them for religious or other reasons may not, in fact, want more of these goods. But from the standpoint of the original position, it is rational for the parties to suppose that they do want a larger share, since in any case they are not compelled to accept more if they do not wish to, nor does a person suffer from a greater liberty.[33]

So if a person is deprived of primary goods, we cannot be sure that his rational life plan will suffer as a result. For he may be deprived of goods that are not necessary for his particular rational life plan. As we saw in our discussion of primary goods above, this lack of fit is quite extensive between primary goods and the rational life plans they are supposed to further. Consider the grass-counter or the aspiring capitalist entrepreneur discussed earlier. How would a loss of political liberty (among the most highly ranked primary goods) affect *their* rational plans of life? We are not entitled to conclude that X's rational life plan has encountered decisive difficulties merely from the fact that he has lost primary goods, even in substantial amounts. The diversity of rational life plans is simply too great to support such an inference.

Furthermore, even if X's rational life plan, in the Rawlsian sense, were undermined by a lack of primary goods, how would that affect his essential interests? For in case (2), X's loss in primary goods goes unaccompanied by severe deprivations. Hence X's *actual* life plan has not been severely affected. X's actual plan has not been hindered by coercive conditions; neither has it suffered any reversal that X, himself, regards as important. Without a severe deprivation, X's loss in primary goods would not have affected X's interests in any way that X himself regards as having great importance.

My account of severe deprivations depends on X's own evaluation of his interests—provided that X has not been subjected to extreme coercive conditions of a kind that would disqualify that evaluation. If X has not been subjected to such coercive conditions—and if he also does not regard the lack of primary goods as a reversal to his actual life plan—then why should such a lack of primary goods be interpreted as affecting his essential interests?

The account of severe deprivations offered here only purports to discriminate consequences destroying X's essential interests from consequences that do not. I have just examined two possible cases where Rawls's theory of primary goods could lead to contrasting conclusions about X's essential interests. In each of these cases, however, it would be possible for shares of primary goods to be *entirely* unrelated to the fate of X's rational life plan, in the Rawlsian sense. Furthermore, that rational life plan, even if it were affected by X's share of primary goods, is only a hypothetical construct. This hypothetical plan may be sufficiently divorced from all of X's actual wants, goals, and aspirations that its failure may leave X, for all practical purposes, unaffected. For both of these reasons, I believe that my account of severe deprivations offers a more adequate interpretation of X's essential interests.

If I am correct in these inferences, then possibilities (IIA) and (IIB) are to be preferred to possibilities (IA) and (IB). This means that whether we reason from the original position or from my proposed version of the cake-cutter's method, the principle of nontyranny would be chosen. In this twofold sense, nontyranny is the principle that would be rationally chosen under fair conditions for choosing moral principles. Although it is incomplete, where this principle renders a judgment, it would be judged superior to the Rawlsian alternative.

14. Conclusion

Throughout this essay I have sought to establish two points: (1) nontyranny is a necessary condition for acceptable principles for social choice, and (2) all principles of the three general kinds commonly discussed—procedural principles, absolute rights, and structural principles—legitimate simple tyranny. If they are applied without exceptions or qualifications, they all violate my proposed necessary condition.

If I am correct on these two points, what follows from the analysis? In particular, what routes are there remaining for the development of morally acceptable principles for social choice?

There are only two possibilities. First, there are principles that will avoid legitimating tyranny because they avoid clearly specifying *any* implications. These principles are "weak" or *prima facie* principles; their implications are weakened by such clauses as "other things being equal" or *ceteris paribus*. Before we can determine what they prescribe, we must know in a given case whether "other things" *are* "equal." We can only know this on an ad hoc basis, however. For if clear specifications could be developed (of when other things are, or are not, equal), then such a principle would no longer be weak. For it could then be fully translated into a new strong principle with clear implications—a new principle that fully specified the conditions under which its prescriptions applied.

So the first way in which a more adequate theory might be developed is through "weak" principles. But weak principles are not, in an important sense, theories at all. Rather, they represent a recourse to ad hoc judgment, on a case-by-case basis, when no theory is available.[1]

Second, there are principles that might avoid legitimating tyranny because they do not belong to any of the three types we have considered. They are not procedural, structural, or absolute rights in form. One way to develop such principles would be to incorporate nontyranny explicitly as a first requirement. Once simple tyranny has been ruled out, two main cases would remain to be decided upon: (a) cases where *every* alternative imposes severe deprivations, and (b) cases where *no* alternative imposes severe deprivations. These are the two situations in which the principle of non-tyranny is silent. If more complete, ultimate criteria are to be invented, then some strategy for these cases must be devised. Perhaps elements of the principles we have already criticized will find a role at this point. Democratic decision rules, structural claims about equality and utilitarianism, individual rights to life or property, might all be invoked—once simple tyranny has been ruled out.

The range of possible nontyrannous principles is unlimited. For there are many issues that nontyranny simply does not settle. It is only a necessary, not a sufficient, condition for morally adequate principles. Hence the framework provided here does not offer a basis for choosing among principles that are *all* nontyrannous. Additional tests or assumptions would be required.

It should be emphasized that were such nontyrannous, ultimate criteria to be devised, it would represent a new departure for political theory. It would represent a radical redirection in the kinds of principles that are receiving serious attention. This essay can be read, in part, as a systematic proposal of such an agenda for political theory.

If a policy would destroy a person's essential interests, if it would deny his subsistence needs, if it would deny him an adequate life chance—when all such deprivations could have been avoided for everyone—then it is tyrannous. This basic principle can be seen as one member in a general family of liberal principles—principles that prohibit harming someone unless avoiding that harm would require harming someone else.

A particularly celebrated member of this family is Mill's "harm principle": "That principle is, that the sole end for which mankind are warranted, individually or collectively, in interfering with the liberty of action of any of their number, is self-protection. That the only purpose for which power can be rightfully exercised over any member of a civilized community, against his will, is to prevent harm to others."[2]

If limiting a person's liberty is accepted as *one* particular kind of harm, then that harm can only be imposed, on Mill's principle, "to prevent harm to others." For this reason, Mill's central conclusion is that actions that are purely "self-regarding"—that do not harm others—cannot be subject to government interference.

Mill's principle differs in important ways from the criterion of nontyranny. It is worth noting the two most obvious differences. First, the *only* actions prohibited are interferences with liberty. But there are many harms—in our sense of severe deprivations—that can be imposed without an "interference" with liberty. For example, X may suffer a severe deprivation through a government's *failure* to act. X may starve unless an emergency effort provides food—or X may burn without fire protection, or he may drown without flood relief. Severe deprivations resulting from government *omissions* may be as terrible as any of those resulting from government commissions. But these omissions would not count as "interferences" with liberty.

Second, the concept of "harm" in Mill's principle is a broad one. It is sufficiently broad that a standard objection to the principle has been that there are few actions that do not harm someone.[3] By contrast, the notion of severe deprivations employed here is restricted to certain especially serious harms.[4] It is only when such severe harms are imposed—when they could be entirely avoided—that the principle judges an act to be tyrannous.

But even though my proposal is substantially different than Mill's principle, the two criteria belong within a general family of principles that allow certain harms to be justified only when *other* harms cannot be avoided. According to Mill's version, interferences with liberty are ruled out unless they "prevent harm to others." According to the criterion of nontyranny, severe deprivations are ruled out unless they prevent other severe deprivations—unless the only *alternatives* are policies that would also impose severe deprivations.[5]

In this way, I believe that nontyranny is an especially compelling version of a familiar kind of principle. It presents, in the starkest form, the common sense of a certain kind of liberalism: Harms—especially serious ones—cannot be justified when they are entirely avoidable for everyone.

If some readers find this principle obvious, so much the better. For it is not offered as a condition that is meant to be either controversial or surprising. What I do believe to be surprising is the fact that virtually every ultimate criterion currently prominent in political theory violates this obvious condition. Principles of a different kind—principles that are not purely procedural, structural, or absolute rights in form—will be required if more adequate theories are to be developed.

Appendix A. An Alternative Construction of the Argument

While I believe that the entire account of severe deprivations offered here is plausible and defensible, it would be reasonable to suppose that certain portions may turn out to be less controversial than others. Skeptics might wish to consider what portions of the argument would be affected if only the least contestable definition were adopted.[1] While I do not believe that such a restriction in the notion of severe deprivations (and hence in the resulting definition of simple tyranny) would be justified, it might be useful to consider its implications for purposes of argument.

Let us distinguish two interpretations of severe deprivations: (a) a narrow interpretation, which only counts as severe deprivations the coercive conditions specified in chapter 5: threats to subsistence needs and denials of an adequate life chance; and (b) the full interpretation, which counts not only all those deprivations in (a), but also the destruction of other essential interests specified in chapter 4.

Throughout our argument thus far, we have employed the full interpretation. Would it have made any difference to our basic conclusions if we had limited ourselves to the narrower view? A related issue is that the very definition of subsistence is subject to varying interpretations. Would it have made any difference if only the most meager claims were interpreted as subsistence needs? In the review of arguments that follows, the reader, if he wishes, may interpret all references to subsistence in the most restrictive sense. It will not affect the results. Let us now examine whether any of our basic conclusions would be affected by adoption of only the narrow interpretation of severe deprivations.

Consider, first, the argument against procedural principles. If a procedural principle is nonunanimous, then there is no reason why severe deprivations imposed on losing coalitions might not affect the subsistence needs or the life chances of those who lose out. For a procedural principle was defined as a criterion that could legitimate *any* action of the government provided it had the support required by the decision rule.

On the other hand, if a procedural principle is unanimous, our argument was that it must be vulnerable to the problem of severe deprivations through *omission*. Clearly, failures to act can produce consequences as terrible as those resulting from any new policy. And there is no reason to believe that failures to act may not affect subsistence needs or life chances. If a group will perish without flood or famine relief (when an abundance of materials is available or could be requisitioned for assistance), it must be simple tyranny, even on the narrow interpretation, if the government fails to act. Similarly, if certain persons will never have an adequate life chance without explicit government intervention (recall our example of the caste system, or the discrimination against persons at the bottom), then it could be tyranny if the government failed to act. And such failures to act are legitimated under unanimous decision rules by the veto of any single individual. In this way, all procedural principles, whether unanimous or nonunanimous, can legitimate tyrannous choices—even if these are interpreted in only the narrow sense.

Now consider our critique of absolute rights theories—theories that prescribe *"never* violate rights." Versions that attempt to offer complete protection against severe deprivations produce inconsistent results;[2] versions that offer only incomplete protection are vulnerable to tyrannous counter-examples.

Consider Nozick's version of absolute rights. As we saw in chapter 9, redistributing food to save the poor would violate the rights of the rich (on his view). But failing to provide food would not count as violating the rights of the poor—although it would impose severe deprivations on them, even in the narrow sense.

Letting the poor starve when there is abundant food counts as a tyrannous choice—on any of our accounts of severe deprivations. Furthermore, the general problem illustrated by this example is not special to Nozick's analysis. Any other version of absolute rights that offered only incomplete protection from severe deprivations would be vulnerable in the same general way: the severe deprivations *not* ruled out by absolute rights would involve no moral issues at all. On this kind of theory, it could never be wrong to choose such a policy imposing severe deprivations—no matter what alternatives it was compared with. Even if it was compared with only trivial alternatives, there could be no moral issue in choosing a policy that imposed severe deprivations when these were not covered by the definition of absolute rights. Any version of an absolute rights theory that maintains consistency must be subject to this objection.

To see the vulnerability of structural principles to tyranny—even on the narrow interpretation—we have only to return to our example of the caste system. For any structural principle must be indifferent to the operation of a caste system (or of racial discrimination, or of other causal factors) that ensures that those who start at the bottom always remain at the bottom. For structural principles are formulated in terms of the anonymous structure of payoffs to positions. They have no place for questions about how the persons who are assigned to positions at one time compare to the persons assigned to positions at another. Hence any structural principle must be insensitive to the continuing operation of factors that deprive those at the bottom of their chance to rise to higher positions. Thus any structural principle must be insensitive to their being denied an adequate life chance. When given the choice between *structurally identical* alternatives—some of which impose deprivations in this way and some of which do not—all such principles must be entirely indifferent. For according to such principles this kind of severe deprivation raises no moral issue at all. Imposing such deprivations would thus be legitimated by any structural principle.

This brief review suggests that it would make no difference to our basic conclusions if the narrower interpretation of severe deprivations were adopted. However, I believe that the broader interpretation, justified by our account in Part One, is more adequate.[3] I have examined the narrower view only to show that my three critical arguments do not depend on any eccentricities in the definition of life plans and essential interests offered in chapter 4. The severe deprivations defined there could be entirely ignored and our critique of the three general kinds of principles would still yield the same basic conclusions.

Appendix B. More on Maximin and the Guaranteed Minimum

In chapter 13 I argued that maximin was too strong a conclusion to draw based on the three features outlined by Rawls. I argued that the conclusion that was warranted, instead, was a guaranteed minimum.

The relationship among these principles can be seen in the four figures presented here illustrating the two-person case.[1]

In each case, the first "L" shaped curve defines a quadrant of points —any point within such a quadrant would give everyone at least "Z" primary goods. *Any* point within such a northeast quadrant would thus satisfy Rawls's stated assumptions. How points within that quadrant are to be evaluated is an entirely open question.

One possible way, of course, is provided by Rawls's maximin proposal. Indifference curves illustrating maximin are offered in Figure B.1. Maximin would rank points in the quadrant by preferring any point on a higher "L" shaped curve to any point on a lower one.

But there are innumerable other ways in which points within the northeast quadrant might be ranked. For example, Figure B.2 illustrates a utilitarian approach. After everyone has been provided with at least "Z," points that offer a higher total (points on a higher diagonal) are preferred. Figure B.3, to add a third example, illustrates equality—within the northeast quadrant. After everyone has been ensured at least "Z," points are preferred according to how close they are to the 45° line. Lastly, Figure B.4 illustrates a proposal that would simply rank the possibilities according to how they benefit person A.

The crucial fact is that *all* of these proposals (along with any other possible scheme for evaluating points within the northeast, "Z," quadrant) have an equivalent claim on the stated assumptions. They all would ensure everyone at least "Z" primary goods—satisfying the requirements of the three features.

For this reason, while maximin satisfies the assumptions, it is far from a *unique* solution. Hence Rawls is mistaken to offer it as the one solution that would resolve the "priority problem." There are innumerable other principles that, on the stated assumptions, must be *at least as good.*

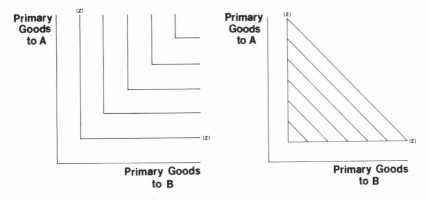

Figure B.1.

Figure B.2.

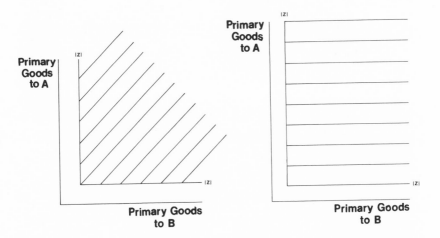

Figure B.3.

Figure B.4.

Appendix C. Structural Principles and Time

My analysis of structural principles in chapter 10 might be objected to on the grounds that a principle employing "fair equal opportunity" as a primary good cannot be "structural" in my proposed sense. For if we know that a person has his share of fair equal opportunity, does that not tell us something about his payoffs at some other time, before or after? Persons cannot, for example, have fair equal opportunity and always remain at the bottom. Hence such principles would violate the requirement, in chapter 10, that payoffs be "temporally independent."

While I believe that equal opportunity might be formulated so that it cannot be included as a payoff in a structural principle, Rawls's version does not have this property. Fair equal opportunity in his sense falls within my argument.

For as I noted in discussing the special conception in chapter 13, fair equal opportunity would not prevent those who have not, in the first place, developed skills and motivation from remaining at the bottom. It is only those "who are at the same level of talent and ability, and have the same willingness to use them" who "should have the same prospects of success regardless of their initial place in the social system."[1]

This definition does not require equal chances to *acquire* skills and motivation, regardless of social class. While Rawls adds that the school system should attempt to "even out class barriers" in the acquisition of "cultural knowledge and skills,"[2] even this requirement does not follow from the definition of fair equal opportunity itself (as quoted above or in this formula): "That those with similar abilities and skills should have similar life chances. . . . In all sectors of society there should be roughly equal prospects of culture and achievement *for those similarly motivated and endowed* [Emphasis added]."[3]

This does not mean that everyone must have the same prospect of *becoming* "similarly motivated and endowed." As Rawls candidly admits, "Even the willingness to make an effort, to try, and so to be deserving in the ordinary sense is itself dependent upon happy family and social circumstances."[4]

The key point is that those who have different motivations and abilities will have different life chances—even if they have had different opportunities, in the first place, to *develop* abilities and motivations.[5]

Hence it is possible, on this interpretation, for a person to have his share of fair equal opportunity and, nevertheless, to be prevented from having prospects of rising above the bottom by a nexus of causal factors affecting the development of motivation and skills in the first place.

A related complexity about time arises if one broadens the account of structural principles to include *intertemporal* utility functions. Suppose that we consider a person's utility to be a function, not only of his presently experienced utility, but also of the utility he has experienced in the past and the utility he can expect to experience in the future. Structural principles defined in terms of such intertemporal utility functions would also be subject to my argument. For if the situations corresponding to X and Y in our counter-examples in chapter 10 are all formulated in terms of such intertemporal utility functions, then the argument proceeds precisely as before. The calculations must, of course, be performed at a given point in time and given reasonable assessments of the utilities each person can expect under each of the policies being compared. So long as it is possible for the same person to have a high position in the matrix of intertemporal utility functions under policy X, and a low position in the matrix under policy Y, the conditions necessary for the argument are satisfied. In our example on page 84, I_2 may be at the top position under X, but if the status quo is changed to situation Y, I_2 may then suffer such a severe change in his (present and expected future) utilities that he moves to the bottom in the matrix of intertemporal utilities. So long as such changes are theoretically possible, my argument holds for such variations of the utilitarian doctrine.

Notes

Chapter 1

1. It is worth emphasizing that this argument is directed at *criteria* for legitimacy. The claim is that various criteria are defective because they would legitimate tyranny. It does not follow from this argument that any particular state that happens to commit an act of tyranny is, by that fact, necessarily illegitimate or deserving of disobedience. My only claim is that those criteria that would legitimate tyrannous choices must be inadequate as ideals for social choice. The argument is directed at criteria; only via those criteria does the argument have implications for the legitimacy or illegitimacy of particular states. See chapter 7 in this volume.

2. The facts of this case are well known. Concerning the popularity of the expulsion, see these accounts in the *New York Times:* 20 August 1972, p. 1, col. 6; 12 October 1972, p. 46, col. 2. For the robberies, beatings, and apparent murders, see the *New York Times,* 12 November 1972, p. 21, col. 1. For the large number of citizens made stateless by the Ugandan authorities, see the *New York Times,* 10 October 1972, p. 2, col. 4.

3. Robert Nozick, *Anarchy, State and Utopia* (New York: Basic Books, 1974), pp. ix, 27-33, 57-58. For a more extensive discussion of Nozick's theory and its vulnerability to tyranny, see chapter 9 in this volume.

4. By particular groups of persons, I mean either named persons or persons in specifiable institutional roles.

5. This classification is similar to Hanna Pitkin's distinction between "procedural" criteria ("those which concern the institutional structure and political functioning of the government, the way it makes decisions and takes actions") and "substantive" criteria ("the substance of what the government does—whether it pursues good, benevolent, justifiable policies"). See Hanna Pitkin, "Obligation and Consent," *Philosophy, Politics and Society,* 4th ser., ed. Peter Laslett, W.G. Runciman, and Quentin Skinner (Oxford: Basil Blackwell, 1972), pp. 44-85. These quotations are from p. 69. This distinction is also reminiscent of Wolheim's distinction between "direct principles" ("Murder is wrong"; "Birth control is permissible") and "oblique principles" ("What is commanded by the sovereign ought to be done"; "What is willed by the people is right"). See Richard Wollheim, "A Paradox in the Theory of Democracy," *Philosophy, Politics and Society,* 2nd ser., ed. Peter Laslett and W.G. Runciman (Oxford: Basil Blackwell, 1962), p. 85.

6. John Rawls, *A Theory of Justice* (Cambridge: Harvard University Press, 1971).

7. This principle has been proposed in two articles: "Maximin Justice and an Alternative Principle of General Advantage," *American Political Science Review* 69, no. 2 (June 1975): 630-47; and "A Principle of Simple Justice," in *Philosophy, Politics and Society,* 5th ser., ed. Peter Laslett and James Fishkin (Oxford: Basil Blackwell/New Haven, Conn.: Yale University Press, 1979).

8. I adopt the notion of "goods" from economics: "By definition, a larger collection of goods gives more satisfaction than a smaller collection. . . . The abstract concept of 'good' can only be applied to things in the real world if it is true that more things give more satisfaction than fewer things." I. M. D. Little, *A Critique of Welfare Economics,* 2nd ed. (Oxford: Oxford University Press, 1957), p. 16. By "more satisfaction" Little simply means that more is "preferred." There is something, in other words, that individuals have shares or amounts of such that more is preferred. However, by this definition of goods, I do not wish to rule out ideal-regarding theories. Hence if the theory prescribes that each individual should rationally want more goods—whether or not he actually does—then such a theory could be structural in my sense provided that it satisfied the rest of the criterion.

9. For a discussion of the standard measures of equality, see Amartya K. Sen, *On Economic Inequality* (New York: Norton, 1973), ch. 3.

10. Rawlsian primary goods include liberty, equal opportunity, and income and wealth. See Rawls, *Theory of Justice,* pp. 60-65, 90-95. For some difficulties in Rawls's account of primary goods, see my "Justice and Rationality: Some Objections to the Central Argument in Rawls's Theory," *American Political Science Review* 69, no. 2 (June 1975): 615-29.

11. Nozick, *Anarchy,* p. 28.

Chapter 2

1. Robert A. Dahl, *A Preface to Democratic Theory* (Chicago: University of Chicago Press, 1956), p. 124.

2. Henry Steele Commager, *Majority Rule and Minority Rights* (Gloucester, Mass.: Peter Smith, 1958), p. 5.

3. Clinton Rossiter, *The Political Thought of the American Revolution* (New York: Harcourt, Brace and World, 1963), ch. 4.

4. From a comment of Jefferson half a century later, quoted in Rossiter, *Political Thought,* p. 64. For an account of the continuities between the political theory of the Declaration of Independence and that of the Constitution, see Martin Diamond, "The Revolution of Sober Expectation," in *The American Revolution: Three Views* (New York: American Brands, 1975), pp. 57-85. See also two more recent studies of the Declaration of Independence: Morton White, *The Philosophy of the American Revolution* (New York: Oxford University Press, 1978), and Garry Wills, *Inventing America* (Garden City, N.Y.: Doubleday, 1978).

5. Dahl concludes that this is the definition actually operative in the argument. Dahl notes that in the *Federalist* (no. 47), Madison offers another explicit definition: "'The accumulation of all powers, legislative, executive, and judiciary, in the same hands, whether of one, a few, or many, may justly be pronounced the very definition of tyranny. [But this] . . . explicit definition has been derived . . . by the insertion of an empirical premise, i.e., the accumulation of all powers in the same hands would lead to severe deprivations of natural rights and hence to tyranny" (see Dahl, *Preface,* p. 6). I find Dahl's account entirely persuasive on this point and, throughout this essay, I treat "every severe deprivation of a natural right" as the Madisonian definition of tyranny.

6. Dahl, *Preface,* p. 6.

7. No. 51. Clinton Rossiter, ed., *The Federalist Papers* (New York: New American

Library, 1961), p. 323. While Madison used the word *injustice* rather than *tyranny* in this passage, the tyranny of the majority was clearly his concern. In fact, the passage was later cited by Toqueville in his discussion of the "tyranny" of the majority. (See Alexis de Tocqueville, *Democracy in America* [New York: Anchor Books, 1969], p. 260.)

8. Dahl, *Preface*, p. 90.

9. The "republican principle" of majority rule was considered an expression of political equality. See Dahl, *Preface*, p. 31.

10. Ibid., p. 10.

11. Ibid., p. 7.

12. Rossiter cites various expressions of the "American consensus" on rights. One of them emphasizes life, liberty, and property; another includes rights to self-government, trial by jury, and freedom of the press; the most famous, of course, are the "unalienable rights" of the Declaration of Independence—"Life, Liberty, and the pursuit of Happiness." It should be obvious that any of these formulations, when applied to the Madisonian definition of tyranny, is subject to the blind-alley problem discussed in this chapter. See Rossiter, *Political Thought*, ch. 4.

13. For further discussion of blind-alley situations, see chapter 9.

14. For an interesting discussion of "moral blind alleys," see Thomas Nagel, "War and Massacre," in *War and Moral Responsibility,* ed. Marshall Cohen, Thomas Nagel, and Thomas Scanlon (Princeton, N.J.: Princeton University Press, 1974), pp. 3-24. Nagel admits that if one assumes that "ought implies can," then a moral blind alley is a considerable embarassment for a theory (for it leads to contradictory results). However, his own position, he admits, is subject to such a blind alley. He attempts to defend it by sacrificing the assumption that "ought implies can." In this essay, on the other hand, I preserve the "ought implies can" assumption throughout. See note 7 to chapter 9.

15. Suppose A and B are the only alternative policies in a given situation. If we are in a blind alley where (1) "A is wrong" and (2) "B is wrong" are both true, we arrive at an inconsistency as follows. Let us assume that "A is wrong" commits us (by the very definition of wrong) to the proposition (3) "Not-A is right." In other words, if it is wrong to do A, then it must be right to do something other than A. But in this simple situation "Not-A" is the same as B. So by (3) we get "B is right" and in (2) above, we assumed "B is wrong."

16. Dahl, *Preface*, ch. 1.

17. Ibid., p. 92. This discussion concerns Dahl's views at the time of the *Preface* (1956). I understand that his position on these issues has changed. His current account of criteria for evaluating democracy can be found in "Procedural Democracy," in *Philosophy, Politics and Society,* 5th ser., ed. Peter Laslett and James Fishkin (Oxford: Basil Blackwell/New Haven, Conn.: Yale University Press, 1979).

18. These figures are reproduced from pages 98 and 99 of Dahl's *Preface.*

19. Ibid., p. 99.

Chapter 3

1. See chapter 6. I would like to thank Douglas Rae for many suggestions which improved my discussion of "simple tyranny."

2. I assume that any notion X has of his own interests must be counted among his preferences. *Paternalism* has often been used in a more restricted sense to refer to interferences with a person's liberty for his own good. I use it in a broader sense, to refer to *judgments* about X's interests that X himself disagrees with. See Gerald Dworkin, "Paternalism," *The Monist* 56, no. 1 (January 1972): 64-84.

3. Brian Barry, *Political Argument* (London: Routledge & Kegan Paul, 1965), pp. 38-

40. Barry considers various ways of drawing this distinction. Compare, for example, the version on page 38 with that on page 40.

4. Lionel Robbins, "Interpersonal Comparisons of Utility: A Comment," *Economic Journal* 48, no. 192 (1938): 635-41, 636. Robbins attributed this story to Sir Henry Maine. For discussions of the spell that this brief statement cast over economics, see, for example, I. M. D. Little, *A Critique of Welfare Economics,* 2nd ed. (Oxford: Oxford University Press, 1957), ch. 4; and Maurice Dobb, *Welfare Economics and the Economics of Socialism* (Cambridge: At the University Press, 1969), ch. 5.

5. Robbins, "Interpersonal Comparisons," p. 636.

6. Ibid., p. 637 (emphasis added).

7. For a discussion of the way X's "satisfaction" and X's "utility" have both been reduced in modern welfare economics to mean no more than that X is "in a chosen position," see Little, *Critique,* chs. 2 and 3.

8. Robbins, "Interpersonal Comparisons," p. 637.

9. I adapt this analogy from a discussion in Little, *Critique,* pp. 51-52.

10. Ibid., p. 120. While there is at least some hyperbole in this statement, the basic point is, I believe, an important one.

11. Recall that if X has a conception of his own interests, then that must count as *at least* one of his preferences, aims, or desires.

12. See John Rawls, *A Theory of Justice* (Cambridge: Harvard University Press, 1971), pp. 90-95, 407-24.

13. Ibid.

14. Ibid., p. 408.

15. Ibid., p. 421.

16. Rawls classifies the theory as ideal regarding (ibid., pp. 326-27). Barry, however, while employing a different version of the distinction than the one employed here, and while focusing on a different portion of the theory than the one discussed here, classifies it as a "want-regarding conception at one remove." See Brian Barry, *The Liberal Theory of Justice* (Oxford: Oxford University Press, 1973), p. 22.

17. Rawls, *Theory of Justice,* p. 421 (emphasis added).

18. For a more recent attempt to deal with this problem, see his "Fairness to Goodness," *Philosophical Review* 84 (October 1975): 536-54.

19. He must be better off with more liberty and less money, say, than with more money and less liberty—regardless of his own preferences in the matter.

20. See James S. Fishkin, "Justice and Rationality: Some Objections to the Central Argument in Rawls's Theory," *American Political Science Review* 69, no. 2 (June 1975): 615-29. See also chapter 14 in this book.

Chapter 4

1. Brian Barry, *Political Argument* (London: Routledge & Kegan Paul, 1965), p. 63. In the discussion that follows, I treat "wants" and "preferences" synonymously.

2. E.J. Mishan, *Welfare Economics: An Assessment* (Amsterdam: North-Holland Publishing, 1969), pp. 34-35.

3. Following Barry in the quotation cited earlier in the chapter, I will allow inclusion of preferences concerning one's most immediate family within the private-regarding, rather than the public-regarding, classification. A different formula for drawing a distinction quite similar to this private/public-regarding distinction can be found in Bernard Williams's notion of an "I-desire." See "Egoism and Altruism" in his *Problems of the Self* (Cambridge: At the University Press, 1973), pp. 250-65.

4. Dahl, however, sometimes discusses intensity in a way that implies that the fundamental phenomenon is "sensate intensity." See *A Preface to Democratic Theory* (Chicago: University of Chicago Press, 1956), pp. 121-23. For a discussion of the various ways *intensity* has been used in democratic theory, see Douglas Rae and Michael Taylor, "Some Ambiguities in the Concept of Intensity," *Polity* 1 (1969): 297-308.

5. Rawls argues that the rational self-interest of anyone is in furthering his rational plan of life. Since primary goods are held to be essential for *any* rational plan—and this is all that an agent in the original position can know about his particular rational plan—it is rational for him to choose so as to guarantee the maximum share of primary goods. It is worth noting that the "thin theory of the good" (the only information about an agent's interests available in the original position) holds that primary goods are to be valued *because* they are necessary to further rational life plans. It is their instrumental connection to rational life plans that provides the rationale for why we should, in the first place, value "primary goods" (such as liberty, fair opportunity, and income and wealth). See Rawls's account of the thin theory in *A Theory of Justice* (Cambridge: Harvard University Press, 1971), pp. 395-99.

6. Ibid., p. 408. Rawls says he borrows this idea from Royce.

7. Ibid., p. 409.

8. "A happy life is not one taken up with deciding whether to do this or that. . . . It is not inconceivable that an individual, or even a whole society, should achieve happiness moved entirely by spontaneous motivation." Ibid., p. 423.

9. I borrow the term *projects* from Bernard Williams, "A Critique of Utilitarianism," in J. J. C. Smart and Bernard Williams, *Utilitarianism: For and Against* (Cambridge: At the University Press, 1973), especially chapter 5.

10. The "courses of action" referred to here are those that are connected to the private-regarding preferences to which X is committed.

11. This definition assumes that X must have more than one private-regarding preference. I maintain that assumption in the discussion that follows. Of course, normally, a person may be expected to have a tremendous variety of private-regarding preferences. However, there is the theoretical possibility of a kind of eccentric life plan that is so fanatically preoccupied with one private-regarding preference that the person has *no* other private-regarding preferences whatsoever. For this bizarre case, an alternative formulation for (b) in (5) would be required. One possibility worth considering is as follows: The criterion for the decisive defeat of such a fanatically monochromatic life plan is that it is decisively defeated if X suffers a reversal so severe that X no longer regards the plan as worth continuing.

12. See the dilemma concerning "integrity" in Bernard Williams's "A Critique of Utilitarianism," chapters 3 and 5.

13. See chapter 11. In the Ugandan examples posed in the Introduction, I assume that the deprivation imposed on the Asians involves more than the loss of property. For their expulsion ruptures an entire way of life. It is for this reason that it would be plausible to suppose that forced exile would constitute a severe deprivation in the precise sense proposed here. Of course, it might be objected that they do not actually turn out to care. But if they *do* care intensely (as it is surely plausible to imagine that they would), then those cases offer counterexamples that fit the definition of tyranny.

14. I do not, by any means, wish to claim that interpersonal comparisons of intensity are impossible. Surely there are many cases in which we can confidently make them in at least a rough way. They become problematical, however, when great precision is required. My claim here is merely that any want-regarding theory must respond to the difficulty either (1) by offering an account of how interpersonal comparisons of intensity are to be

made, or (2) by demonstrating that such an account is not required. I have taken the latter strategy here. For strong assertions that *some* interpersonal comparisons of utility (or of the intensity of preference) can be made, see I. M. D. Little, *A Critique of Welfare Economics* (Oxford: Oxford University Press, 1957), p. 53; and William J. Baumol, *Economic Theory and Operations Analysis,* 4th ed. (Englewood Cliffs, N. J.: Prentice-Hall, 1977), p. 526. Particular schemes can be found in Burton Weisbrod, "Income Redistribution Effects and Benefit-Cost Analysis," in *Problems in Public Expenditure Analysis,* ed. Samuel Chase, Jr. (Washington, D. C.: Brookings Institution, 1967), pp. 177-213; and Amartya K. Sen, *On Economic Inequality* (New York: Norton, 1973), pp. 13-16.

15. Note that Dworkin's proposal is not that rights always trump. As long as a right has sufficient "weight" to override *some* goal, then it can be counted as a right. Even the most fundamental right can be outweighed sometimes by other considerations. If this is "taking rights seriously," one wonders why Dworkin did not choose to take them *more* seriously. Ronald Dworkin, *Taking Rights Seriously* (Cambridge: Harvard University Press, 1977). For the minimum "weight" of a right see page 92. For the sense in which "rights trump goals" see chapters 6 and 7.

It would not be inappropriate to formulate the moral claim involved in severe deprivations as a "right." One has a *prima facie* right not to suffer severe deprivations and a strong or inviolable right not to be tyrannized. (See chapter 9 herein for a discussion of how this kind of right differs from the "absolute rights" discussed there.) If these claims are formulated as "rights," then they are taken more "seriously" here than are the "rights" in Dworkin's theory.

Chapter 5

1. James C. Scott, *The Moral Economy of the Peasant: Rebellion and Subsistence in Southeast Asia* (New Haven, Conn.: Yale University Press, 1976), p. 17.

2. It is "exploitative" by any standards having to do with the proportion taken away by the owner; for the peasant's concern, according to Scott, is more with how much is left than with how much is taken away. See ibid., ch. 1.

3. Barrington Moore, Jr., *Injustice: The Social Bases of Obedience and Revolt* (White Plains, N.Y.: M.E. Sharpe, 1978), ch. 2.

4. However, this difficulty has sometimes been exaggerated. See Scott, *Moral Economy,* p. 191.

5. Ibid., p. 16.

6. Ibid., p. 17.

7. Ibid.

8. George Orwell, *The Road to Wigan Pier* (New York: Harvest Books, 1958), p. 100.

9. For an evaluation of these diets, see: A.B. Atkinson, "Poverty and Income Inequality in Britain," in *Poverty, Inequality and Class Structure,* ed. Dorothy Wedderburn (Cambridge: At the University Press, 1974), pp. 43-70; Peter Townsend, "Poverty as Relative Deprivation: Resources and Style of Living," in Wedderburn's *Poverty, Inequality and Class Structure,* pp. 15-41; Kenneth Keniston and The Carnegie Council on Children, *All Our Children: The American Family Under Pressure* (New York: Harcourt, Brace, Jovanovich, 1977), ch. 2; and Lee Rainwater, *What Money Buys: Inequality and the Social Meanings of Income* (New York: Basic Books, 1974), ch. 3.

10. The 1908 budget was calculated for Fall River, Massachusetts. The comparison is discussed in Rainwater, *What Money Buys,* p. 48.

11. Adam Smith, *An Inquiry into the Nature and Causes of the Wealth of Nations* (New York: Modern Library, 1937), book V, ch. 2, pp. 821-22.

12. Ibid., p. 822.

13. As Townsend notes about persons at a comparable level of poverty: "Their resources are so seriously below those commanded by the average individual or family that they are, in effect, excluded from ordinary living patterns, customs and activities" ("Poverty as Relative Deprivation," p. 15).

14. For a similar argument that the definition of subsistence should include more than the bare minimum for physical survival, see W.G. Runciman, *Relative Deprivation and Social Justice* (Berkeley: University of California Press, 1966), pp. 265-66.

15. Michael Harrington, *The Other America: Poverty in the United States,* rev. ed. (New York: Pelican, 1971), p. 11.

16. Ibid., p. 18.

17. Keniston and The Carnegie Council, *All Our Children,* p. 34.

18. Ibid., p. 45.

19. Samuel Bowles and Herbert Gintis, *Schooling in Capitalist America: Educational Reform and the Contradictions of Economic Life* (New York: Basic Books, 1976), p. 121.

20. Keniston and The Carnegie Council, *All Our Children,* p. 36.

21. Harrington, *Other America,* p. 15.

22. Evidence on such a consensus in various countries is reviewed in Seymour Martin Lipset and Reinhard Bendix, *Social Mobility in Industrial Society* (Berkeley: University of California Press, 1967), pp. 269-76.

23. For an interesting argument that this possibility will never arise see Ralf Dahrendorf, "On the Origin of Social Inequality," in *Philosophy, Politics and Society,* 2nd ser., ed. Peter Laslett and W.G. Runciman (Oxford: Basil Blackwell, 1962), pp. 88-109.

24. See Robert E. Lane, "The Fear of Equality," *Political Ideology: Why the American Common Man Believes What He Does* (New York: Free Press, 1962), pp. 57-81; also Runciman, *Relative Deprivation,* chs. 10 and 11.

25. For an argument in favor of paternalism (both paternalistic judgments and interferences justified by those judgments) in comparable cases, see Gerald Dworkin, "Paternalism," *The Monist* 56, no. 1 (January 1972): 64-84. Note, for example, his discussion of suicide on pp. 81-82.

Chapter 6

1. H. L. A. Hart and A.M. Honoré, *Causation in the Law* (Oxford: Oxford University Press, 1959).

2. Ibid., p. 2.

3. An action may, of course, require a series of physical changes (movements). However, a movement may take place (that is, involuntarily) without any *action* having been performed. For an extended discussion of such issues, see A.I. Melden, *Free Action* (London: Routledge & Kegan Paul, 1961).

4. Hart and Honoré, *Causation,* p. 48.

5. Hart and Honoré specify four conditions for this kind of causation: "(i) In all of them the second actor knows of and understands the significance of what the first actor has said or done; (ii) the first actor's words or deeds are part of the second actor's reasons for acting; (iii) the second actor forms the intention to do the act in question only after the first actor's intervention; (iv) except in the case where the first actor has merely advised the second actor, he intends the second actor to do the act in question" (ibid., pp. 49-50).

6. Ibid., p. 56.

7. Ibid., p. 55.

8. Ibid., p. 56.

9. Joel Feinberg, "The Forms and Limits of Utilitarianism," *Philosophical Review* 76 (July 1967): 368-81, 369. This topic has been much discussed. Some writers, following Sidgwick's distinction between the utility of an action and the utility of the praise of it, have wished to distinguish whether the agent would be *blameworthy* (in terms of probable consequences) from whether he would be wrong (in terms of actual consequences). For similar distinctions between probable and actual consequences, see J. J. C. Smart, "Extreme and Restricted Utilitarianism," reprinted in *Contemporary Utilitarianism,* ed. Michael D. Bayles (New York: Doubleday, 1968), pp. 99-116; and Robert J. Ackermann, "The Consequences," in *Logic and Art: Essays in Honor of Nelson Goodman,* ed. Richard Rudner and Israel Scheffler (Indianapolis, Ind.: Bobbs-Merrill, 1972), pp. 43-57, esp. p. 44. Smart has also distinguished "rational" and "right" actions along similar lines, in "An Outline of a System of Utilitarian Ethics," in J. J. C. Smart and Bernard Williams, *Utilitarianism: For and Against* (Cambridge: At the University Press, 1973), pp. 1-74, esp. p. 47.

10. G. E. M. Anscombe, "The Two Kinds of Error in Action," in *Ethics,* ed. Judith J. Thomson and Gerald Dworkin (New York: Harper & Row, 1968), pp. 279-88, 287.

11. Ibid., p. 287.

12. Ibid., p. 288.

13. In identifying a knowledgeable and impartial assessment of causal connections with one that would be supported by scientific inquiry, I am committed to a nonrelativistic view of science. For a vigorous defense of such a position, see Israel Scheffler, *Science and Subjectivity* (Indianapolis, Ind.: Bobbs-Merrill, 1967). See also the important controversy between Popper and Kuhn in *Criticism and Growth of Knowledge,* ed. Imre Lakatos and Alan Musgrave (Cambridge: At the University Press, 1970).

14. This example was suggested to me by Paul Burstein (of the Yale Department of Sociology) from his study of Israeli society.

15. Consider facts that are "essentially contested." The definition of human life in abortion cases is an obvious recent example. For the notion of essentially contested concepts, see W.B. Gallie, *Philosophy and the Historical Understanding* (London: Chatto & Windus, 1964), pp. 157-91; and John Gray, "On the Contestability of Social and Political Concepts," *Political Theory* 5, no. 3 (August 1977): 331-48.

16. Consider, for example, how dubious causal connections, if admitted, could be used to alter application of "tyranny" to the Nazi case.

17. Quentin Skinner, "'Social Meaning' and the Explanation of Social Action," in *Philosophy, Politics and Society,* 4th ser., ed. Peter Laslett, W.G. Runciman, and Quentin Skinner (Oxford: Basil Blackwell, 1972), pp. 136-57, 143.

18. I first heard a version of this story in Quentin Skinner's lectures at Cambridge in 1972. For a discussion of precisely how the Yoruba beliefs are beyond empirical investigation, see Martin Hollis, "Reason and Ritual," in *Rationality,* ed. Bryan A. Wilson (Oxford: Basil Blackwell, 1970), pp. 221-39.

19. There may, of course, be a time lag in this realization. I set aside the special case in which the person is prevented from the eventual realization by some *other* severe deprivation.

20. In chapter 4 I assumed that a minimal degree of competence is necessary on the part of those forming life plans if we are to employ those plans in defining their essential interests. There are, of course, cases in which a person never develops minimal competence. While paternalistic judgments would also be required for such cases, I do not deal with them here.

21. Robert Nozick, *Anarchy, State and Utopia* (New York: Basic Books, 1974), pp. 74 and 82.

22. Nozick (*Anarchy,* pp. 74-75) states:

Imposing how slight a probability of a harm that violates someone's rights also violates his rights? Instead of one cut-off probability for all harms, perhaps the cut-off probability is lower the more severe the harm. Here one might have the picture of a specified value, the same for all acts, to mark the boundary of rights violation; an action violates someone's rights if its expected harm to him (that is, its probability of harm to him multiplied by a measure of that harm) is greater than, or equal to, the specified value.

23. Charles Fried makes a similar claim. For example, "What is being argued here is that there is a certain level of risk—let us call it the ordinary or background level of risk—which is necessary to allow ordinary activity to take place" (Charles Fried, *An Anatomy of Values* [Cambridge: Harvard University Press, 1970], p. 193).

24. I assume that if revolution is considered as a policy alternative it will usually be reasonable to conclude that it involves serious risks of severe deprivations. Therefore, it will usually be the case that the search for nontyrannous policy alternatives will proceed within some ongoing constitutional system. In most social systems it can also be assumed that violations of the rule of law will involve similar risks.

25. David Braybrooke and Charles E. Lindblom, *A Strategy for Decision: Policy Evaluation as a Social Process* (New York: The Free Press, 1970), pts. 1 and 2.

Chapter 7

1. The phrase, of course, belongs to Herman Kahn. For a discussion of issues it poses in moral philosophy, see Bernard Williams, "A Critique of Utilitarianism," in J. J. C. Smart and Bernard Williams, *Utilitarianism: For and Against* (Cambridge: At the University Press, 1973), p. 92.

2. Rawls's formulation is that ideal theory "assumes strict compliance and works out the principles that characterize a well-ordered society under favorable circumstances." (John Rawls, *A Theory of Justice* [Cambridge: Harvard University Press, 1971], p. 245.) My difficulty with this formulation has to do with ambiguities in the notion of a "well-ordered society": ". . . a society in which everyone accepts and knows that the others accept the same principles of justice, and the basic social institutions satisfy and are known to satisfy these principles" (pp. 453-54). The question is, how demanding is this latter requirement that the basic institutions have to "satisfy" (and be known to satisfy) the proposed principles? When, in other words, is the ideal fully realized? If further improvements are always possible, at what point have the principles been satisfied? It should be obvious that if this requirement is taken too seriously, then the realm of ideal theory can become utopian. The formulation I have proposed, on the other hand, is meant to designate clearly optimistic assumptions, but assumptions that fall short of the more utopian interpretations of the Rawlsian proposal. The basic notions are, however, quite similar, for Rawls specifies both "favorable conditions" and "strict compliance" in the definition cited above.

3. Ibid., p. 127.

4. Ibid., pp. 8-9, 242.

5. This rider would not apply to present conditions that can be traced to tyranny in a *preceding* generation. For a person now living cannot be held to share responsibility in those policies of a previous epoch. While there are interesting questions about present obligations derived from past injustice, I do not believe they fall within the limited scope of the principle of nontyranny. It would never, in other words, be *tyrannous* for a government to fail to rectify an injustice from a *preceding* generation. For a bold argument that *no*

present account whatsoever need be taken of any injustices in *previous* generations, see Peter Laslett, "The Conversation Between the Generations," in *Philosophy, Politics and Society*, 5th ser., ed. Peter Laslett and James Fishkin (Oxford: Basil Blackwell/New Haven, Conn.: Yale University Press, 1979).

6. See Guido Calabresi and Philip Bobbitt, *Tragic Choices: The Conflicts Society Confronts in the Allocation of Tragically Scarce Resources* (New York: W.W. Norton, 1978).

7. David Lyons, *The Forms and Limits of Utilitarianism* (Oxford: Oxford University Press, 1965), p. 19.

8. Ibid., p. 20.

9. Ibid.

10. Rawls, *Theory of Justice*, p. 34.

11. Ibid., p. 39.

12. By "equally good" I mean equally appropriate as moral choices. The same notion is captured in the economist's terminology by saying we should be "indifferent" between the two options.

Chapter 8

1. So a principle of majority rule (provided that it includes such a requirement) may not be invoked to legitimate a change in decision rules away from majority rule—even if that change is approved by majority vote. Procedural principles may be defined with or without such a prohibition on changing the decision rule in the future. Such a clause freezing the decision rule would not prevent tyranny, for as we shall see, tyrannous choices are compatible with *any* of the decision rules we have defined as procedural.

One bizarre possibility perhaps should also be mentioned. Suppose that the decision rule is defined so that the participation of certain particular persons is required. The decision rule is defined so as to mandate the participation of persons X, Y, Z, etc. These persons might then be regarded as protected (by the procedural principle) from any severe deprivations that would prevent their participation. However, such a requirement would not, of course, prevent severe deprivations from being imposed on anyone whose participation was not mandated in this way.

Suppose, to push the example further, that the decision rule is defined in such a way that it requires participation from absolutely everyone—and any alteration of such participation must be regarded as a change in the decision rule by the government. No decision rule with this property has ever, to my knowledge, been seriously proposed. However, I will assume, in this case, that if participation in politics is required, in some way, from *everyone* in the society, then politics must be a small enough part of each (or many) individual's life that he would be vulnerable to severe deprivations in many *other* spheres of life. In other words, whatever the participation required by the decision rule, it would have to be possible for some persons to continue it while suffering severe deprivations that did not touch directly on their political activity. The argument then proceeds as before, for those other severe deprivations can be imposed through omission or commission, depending on the precise decision rule.

Note, furthermore, the many difficulties passed over by this notion of "everyone." Does this include children, criminals, the insane? For an illuminating discussion of who should be included as participating members in the polity, see Robert Dahl's "Procedural Democracy" in *Philosophy, Politics and Society*, 5th ser., ed. Peter Laslett and James Fishkin (Oxford: Basil Blackwell/New Haven, Conn.: Yale University Press, 1979).

2. Joseph Schumpeter, *Capitalism, Socialism and Democracy*, 3d ed. (New York: Harper & Row, 1950), pp. 240, 242.

3. Ibid., p. 242.

4. Robert Paul Wolff, *In Defense of Anarchism* (New York: Harper & Row, 1970), p. 27.

5. Ibid., p. 14.

6. Ibid., p. 23.

7. Wolff admits as much in a later reply to one of his critics. He refers to his earlier claim (that the autonomy of the individual was rendered compatible with the authority of the state by a rule of unanimous direct democracy) as "nonsense." See Robert Paul Wolff, "A Reply to Reiman," in *In Defense of Anarchism,* 2nd ed. (New York: Harper & Row, 1976), p. 88.

8. James Buchanan and Gordon Tullock, *The Calculus of Consent* (Ann Arbor: University of Michigan Press, 1971), p. 64.

9. This is more obviously the case because, according to Buchanan and Tullock, agents at the constitutional convention presuppose an already existing delineation of property rights. Hence a poor person might calculate that his external costs would increase (and not decrease as Buchanan and Tullock hypothesize) as the number required to take action increases—because the rich could more easily block efforts at redistribution under such a decision rule. See Buchanan and Tullock's comments on property rights (*Calculus of Consent,* p. 47 and esp. p. 345, n. 3). This discussion of unanimity has benefited greatly from Douglas Rae's penetrating essay, "The Limits of Consensual Decision," *American Political Science Review* 69, no. 4 (December 1975): 1270-94.

10. Wolff, for example, suggests this no-agreement point: "Since by the rule of unanimity a single negative vote defeats any motion, the slightest disagreement over significant questions will bring the operations of society to a halt. It will cease to function as a political community and fall into a condition of anarchy" (*Anarchism,* p. 24).

11. When consent is defined so that it can be applied universally it may also become vacuous in content. See Hanna Pitkin's criticisms of Tussman in "Obligation and Consent," *Philosophy, Politics and Society,* 4th ser., ed. Peter Laslett, W.G. Runciman, and Quentin Skinner (Oxford: Basil Blackwell, 1972), pp. 44-85.

12. Ibid., p. 66.

13. We have only to substitute the words *failed to prohibit persecution* for *reached the decision to persecute* and the argument can be applied directly to unanimous principles.

Chapter 9

1. Absolute rights theories will vary in their interpretation of this last clause ("as the result of the actions of others"). They may be incomplete, for example, by omitting protection against the results of inactions. Or they may protect only against deliberate harms. Or they may be incomplete in some other way. Complete theories will include protection against all actions by the state connected to severe deprivations—resulting in the inconsistency difficulty discussed here. Incomplete theories will be selective in the protection they offer—resulting in their vulnerability to tyrannous counterexamples discussed here.

2. By *others* I mean persons under other circumstances. The "other" person may even be the same person in some other role or situation. Suppose the alternatives are such that one policy would affect A at work and another would affect him at home. For our purposes, such a case will be handled in the same way as one in which the person at home were B and the person at work, A.

3. Robert Nozick, *Anarchy, State and Utopia* (New York: Basic Books, 1974), pp. 28-32.

4. I have in mind the controversial Reserve Mining Case in Minnesota. However, I

have altered and simplified particulars. The issue there was water pollution produced by taconite tailings that created a danger of asbestos fibers, which are thought to pose risks of cancer. In my adaptation I have assumed that the risk is both less controversial and much more serious.

5. Let us also assume that the costs of the pollution control system are so great that the company could not survive (if it had to operate in that way), even with a loan guarantee.

6. I am indebted to Marie Rogers for originally suggesting this example to me. Whether or not this second example falls outside the bounds of ideal theory depends on the intepretation of "moderate scarcity." For I said that, at the lower end, this meant that everyone's subsistence needs could be secured in that everyone could be provided with the "necessaries" in Adam Smith's sense. Everyone could be secured that level of economic resources and still be subject to the epidemic as it spreads. Furthermore, the spread of the epidemic cannot be attributed to violation of any of the other conditions (that is, it does not result from past violations of the principle or lack of strict compliance with the principle). Nevertheless, if the example is objected to on these grounds, it can be set aside. For the general issue remains: There are cases in which every alternative imposes severe deprivations and an absolute prohibition against imposing severe deprivations will, therefore, lead to contradictory results.

7. Throughout this essay, I assume that "ought implies can." To prescribe "not-A_1" is to presuppose that there is some alternative (or combination of alternatives) that should be performed instead of A_1. But there can be no such alternative in cases of this kind. Nagel makes this point explicit by conceding that if he admits that his position is vulnerable to such blind alleys he must, as a result, sacrifice the assumption that "ought implies can." Thomas Nagel, "War and Massacre," in *War and Moral Responsibility,* ed. Marshall Cohen, Thomas Nagel, and Thomas Scanlon (Princeton, N.J.: Princeton University Press, 1974), pp. 23-24.

8. Absolute rights principles are "strong" in logical form (recall the injunction *"never* violate the rights of anyone"). Hence there is no question that a conflict of strong principles produces a logical contradiction. See my discussion of "strong" principles in chapter 7.

9. Or, the inconsistency might be expressed as the conflict between these two propositions: (1) It is morally required that the government choose A_2, A_3, or . . . A_N; (2) It is not morally required (in fact, it is morally prohibited) that the government choose A_2, A_3, or . . . A_N.

10. An absolute rights formulation might offer less than complete protection against severe deprivations and still rule out every possible alternative for some possible case. Such a formulation would be both inconsistent and subject to tyrannous counterexample. I consider only those subject to the second problem.

11. Nozick, *Anarchy,* p. 29.

12. Ibid., p. 30. Although this particular passage appears in a discussion of the ultraminimal state, the distinction applies generally to the side constraint notion.

13. Ibid., p. 181. This is, of course, a version of Kohlberg's famous moral dilemma. See Lawrence Kohlberg, "From Is to Ought," in T. Mischel, *Cognitive Development and Epistemology* (New York: Academic Press, 1971), pp. 151-235.

14. Nozick, *Anarchy,* p. ix.

15. Ibid.

16. This strategy of selectivity would only succeed if refraining from crossing anyone's boundaries were always an option. Philippa Foot poses a problem for individual choice in which every option would kill someone and such inaction would be impossible (the driver of a runaway railway train who could only steer left or right with dire consequences either way). I do not know whether a similar example could be contrived in which every option

open to the *state* would be a boundary crossing in Nozick's sense. Whether or not such a theory can be formulated consistently, it is still subject to my objection that because of the incompleteness of its protection, it would legitimate tyranny. See Philippa Foot, "The Problem of Abortion and the Doctrine of the Double Effect," in *Moral Problems,* ed. James Rachels (New York: Harper & Row, 1971), pp. 28-41.

17. Nagel, "War and Massacre," p. 9.

18. Ibid., p. 10.

19. Ibid.

20. The precise distinction applied to killing is "between bringing about the death of an innocent person deliberately, either as an end in itself or as a means, and bringing it about as a side effect of something else one does deliberately." Ibid.

21. Such severe deprivations may, of course, be reasonably foreseeable even though they may be an unintended by-product. If, in order to save A, we have to refrain from saving B, this may be reasonably foreseeable even though the effect on B was not the one deliberately intended (see note 19 to this chapter).

22. This must be so for absolute rights theories as we have defined them. Nozick's theory clearly conforms to our definition. Nagel's position is more ambiguous; he offers only "a somewhat qualified defense of absolutism" ("War and Massacre," p. 6), for he wishes to leave room for utilitarianism as well. My comments apply to the "absolutist" position he defines. I leave open the question of whether it applies to the more ambiguous position he is willing to endorse as his own.

23. I formulate A_2 in this way in order to point out that if there were such an A_2 alternative that imposed *no* severe deprivations on anyone, the absolute rights principle would be indifferent between such an A_2 and the A_1 alternative already described. This example should *not* be taken to suggest that a principle avoiding tyranny would only permit such food or medical assistance to be offered if it could be done without imposing severe deprivations. See the discussion of structural principles in chapter 10.

24. Recall my argument in chapter 7 that if a principle rates the tyrannous and nontyrannous alternatives as equally good, then it supports a tyrannous choice in a way that counts as a decisive counterexample.

Chapter 10

1. This category is similar to Nozick's notion of an "end-state principle." My grounds for criticism (that such principles would legitimate tyranny) are, of course, different. See Robert Nozick, *Anarchy, State and Utopia* (New York: Basic Books, 1974), pp. 153-55.

2. I adopt the notion of "goods" from economics: "By definition, a larger collection of goods gives more satisfaction than a smaller collection. . . . The abstract concept of 'good' can only be applied to things in the real world if it is true that more things give more satisfaction than fewer things" (I. M. D. Little, *A Critique of Welfare Economics,* 2nd ed. [Oxford: Oxford University Press, 1957], p. 16). By "more satisfaction" Little simply means that more is preferred or would be chosen. There is something, in other words, that individuals have shares or amounts of such that more is preferred. Several points should be noted:

a. The amounts of such goods will usually be susceptible to cardinal measurement. Some structural principles, however, can determine choices even when the payoffs are only measured ordinally. See, for example, Rawls's position that maximin requires only ordinal rankings (because anything that makes the lowest ranked person better off is preferred). See John Rawls, *A Theory of Justice* (Cambridge: Harvard University Press, 1971), pp. 91-92.

b. By this definition of goods, I do not mean to rule out ideal-regarding accounts of payoffs in structural theories. Hence if a theory prescribes that each individual *should* rationally prefer more of certain "goods" susceptible to measurement, then those goods count as payoffs for these purposes.

c. Welfare itself can be counted as a good (if it is susceptible to measurement), since more is always preferred.

d. If a plausible index of Rawlsian primary goods could be constructed, then rights and liberties could be included within the payoffs of a structural theory.

3. In his original formulation, Rae offered this proposal as an alternative to Rawls's general maximin proposal. In a later version, Rae appears to have qualified the proposal so that perhaps it is no longer intended as an ultimate criterion. See Douglas W. Rae, "Maximin Justice and an Alternative Principle of General Advantage," *American Political Science Review* 69, no. 2 (June 1975): 630-47; idem, "A Principle of Simple Justice," in *Philosophy, Politics and Society,* 5th ser., ed. Peter Laslett and James Fishkin (Oxford: Basil Blackwell/New Haven, Conn.: Yale University Press, 1979).

4. There are some alternatives that serve general advantage (advantaging some strata and making none worse off) and also increase equality. There are also some alternatives that serve equality—and not general advantage—but that, nevertheless, increase the total.

5. The argument does not require this assumption that the Y' alternatives are always slightly inferior, on structural grounds, to the Y alternatives. Suppose that the Y' alternatives are always structurally identical to the Y options—but that Y' always differs in this way only: through affirmative action, groups at the bottom have prospects of rising to higher positions. Even if this more optimistic assumption (that Y' is always as good as Y on structural grounds) were made, the same result would follow. For *any* structural principle would still legitimate a pattern in which Y was always chosen. For it would always rate Y and Y' precisely equal. There would be no *moral* issue in choosing Y rather than Y'. Structural principles are formulated so that the affirmative action benefits must count for nothing when considered by themselves.

6. My claim about absolute rights principles is that all of those that avoid the inconsistency discussed in chapter 9 legitimate tyranny.

Chapter 11

1. See, for example, E.J. Mishan, *Economics for Social Decisions: Elements of Cost-Benefit Analysis* (New York: Praeger, 1973); and M.W. Jones-Lee, *The Value of Life: An Economic Analysis* (Chicago: University of Chicago Press, 1976).

2. Especially cogent analyses of the original proposals and the vast literature they have produced can be found in the following: I. M. D. Little, *A Critique of Welfare Economics,* 2nd ed. (Oxford: Oxford University Press, 1957); E.J. Mishan, *Welfare Economics: An Assessment* (Amsterdam: North-Holland Publishing, 1969); and Maurice Dobb, *Welfare Economics and the Economics of Socialism* (Cambridge: At the University Press, 1969).

3. Except, of course, for those points that determine, in turn, a northeast quadrant with respect to point 1.

4. Cited in Little, *Critique,* p. 92. This argument originally appeared in J. R. Hicks, "The Rehabilitation of Consumers' Surplus," *Review of Economic Studies* (1940-41): 108-16.

5. A change in production factors may shift the utility possibility locus so that two curves cross. In such cases (where they cross between two points that are being compared) the Kaldor-Hicks criterion will produce contradictory results (prescribing each of the two points as better than the other), and Scitovsky's formulation will say nothing. In all other

cases the two versions agree. See Little, *Critique,* pp. 96-107; and Dobb, *Welfare Economics,* pp. 84-85.

6. William J. Baumol, *Economic Theory and Operations Analysis,* 4th ed. (Englewood Cliffs, N.J.: Prentice-Hall, 1977), p. 530.

7. Little, *Critique,* p. 87.

8. Ibid., p. 90. If A can "overcompensate" B, then A could fully compensate B and be better off than before the change.

9. See, for example, Burton Weisbrod, "Income Redistribution Effects and Benefit-Cost Analysis," in *Problems in Public Expenditure Analysis,* ed. Samuel Chase, Jr. (Washington, D.C.: Brookings Institution, 1967), pp. 177-213.

Chapter 12

1. John Rawls, *A Theory of Justice* (Cambridge: Harvard University Press, 1971), p. 85. There are more complex variations of this "cut and choose" procedure that are invulnerable to collusion and deception. But these safeguards are not necessary for the thought experiment explored here.

2. The cake-cutter's analogy is offered as a model of "perfect procedural justice," while the original position is said to exemplify "pure procedural justice." There are, I believe, difficulties in Rawls's effort to distinguish the two in this way. The crucial difference between the "perfect" procedure and the "pure" one is that the former procedure has "an independent criterion" for the appropriate outcome. Rawls believes this to be true of the cake-cutter because of the obviousness of equality as a solution. He denies, however, that this is true of the original position by classifying it as a case of "pure procedural justice." I believe this undermines his claim that a process of "reflective equilibrium" supports the original position. For one characteristic of that process was that we are to "work from both ends." We examine not only whether the conditions of choice are appealing but also whether the results conform to our "considered judgments." It is precisely because we have an "independent criterion" for the results of the original position (in these "considered judgments") that we can claim to have reached "reflective equilibrium." But if we have an independent criterion, then the original position cannot be "pure procedural justice." It does not appear to differ, in these respects, from the "perfect procedural justice" of the cake-cutter's analogy. For Rawls's account of perfect and pure procedural justice, see *Theory of Justice,* pp. 85-86. For his claim about the original position, see pp. 120, 136. For reflective equilibrium, see pp. 20, 48-51.

3. This argument is presented in greater detail in my "Justice and Rationality: Some Objections to the Central Argument in Rawls's Theory," *American Political Science Review* 69, no. 2 (June 1975): 615-29.

4. Maximin is the outcome in the case of the "general conception." A more complex result (the "two principles") follows in the case of the special conception.

5. Rawls argues that if he gambles, he would choose the principle of average utility. Rawls, however, believes the more "conservative" strategy of maximin is rational in the original position. See my discussion in chapter 13.

6. Rawls says: "The contract doctrine is purely hypothetical: if a conception of justice would be agreed to in the original position, its principles are the right ones to apply. It is no objection that such an understanding has never been nor ever will be entered into" (*Theory of Justice,* p. 167).

7. In formulating the problem as one that concerns criteria for *policy* choice, I assume that I am, indirectly, also formulating the problem of criteria for *constitutional* choice. The criterion of nontyranny applies to both: it requires (a) that a government not commit

acts of simple tyranny in its policy choices, and (b) that the constitutional order within which that government functions is one that makes (a) possible.

8. The order of choice before I_1 may be specified, for these purposes, as random or determined by lot. A similar specification should be supplied for the division of the cake.

9. Amartya K. Sen, *Collective Choice and Social Welfare* (San Francisco: Holden Day, 1970), p. 149.

10. Mackie distinguishes the version of universalizability where A imagines himself in B's place with B's preference from the version where A imagines himself in B's place with A's preferences. I believe that the Hindu-Moslem case shows the absurdity of the latter version. See J.L. Mackie, *Ethics: Inventing Right and Wrong* (New York: Penguin, 1977), ch. 4. Mackie argues that these versions of "universalizability" are not clearly distinguished in R.M. Hare's famous account in *Freedom and Reason* (Oxford: Oxford University Press, 1963).

11. Rawls, *Theory of Justice*, p. 152.

Chapter 13

1. John Rawls, *A Theory of Justice* (Cambridge: Harvard University Press, 1971), section 8.

2. This paragraph assumes that we are willing to restrict the comparison to these four combinations of Rawls's proposals and my own. See the paragraph immediately following for the problem posed by other decision procedures.

3. See the comments following concerning the dependence of the original position on the three features. Without the three features the result is indeterminate. With the three features, the issue seems to be determined by unjustified assumptions.

4. These include: (a) the perfectly sympathetic and impartial spectator of the classical utilitarians, (b) the version of the original position that includes envy so as to yield a principle of equality, and (c) the version that incorporates probabilistic calculations so as to yield average utility.

5. Rawls, *Theory of Justice*, section 21.

6. Ibid., p. 154.

7. Ibid.

8. Ibid.

9. This can be seen from the following: "His expectation is defined . . . by a weighted sum of utilities of representative individuals, that is, by the expression $\Sigma\, p_i u_i$ where p_i is the likelihood of his achieving the ith position, and u_i the utility of the corresponding man" (ibid., pp. 164-65). Now if an agent in the original position reasons according to the principle of insufficient reason that he has an equal likelihood of turning out to be any particular individual, then he may compute p_i in each case by determining the fraction that the ith person represents of the total population (in the case of one individual, $1/n$). His total prospect is thus

$$1/n\, u_1 + 1/n\, u_2 + \ldots + 1/n\, u_n \text{ or } \Sigma\, u_i/n$$

The above expression, however, is identical to the average utility, for since the total utility must be $\Sigma\, u_i$ and the total number of persons is n, the average utility for a given society must represent the total utility divided by the number of its persons, or $\Sigma\, u_i/n$. Hence, the society that maximizes the average utility also maximizes the expectation of total utility for any individual in the original position— provided that one assumes he has an equal likelihood of turning out to be anyone. See ibid., especially pp. 164-65.

10. In this discussion of the three features, I have borrowed from my argument in

"Justice and Rationality: Some Objections to the Central Argument in Rawls's Theory," *American Political Science Review* 69, no. 2 (June 1975): 615-29.

11. Rawls, *Theory of Justice*, p. 93.

12. In the thought experiment defined by the cake-cutter's procedure, everyone is assumed to act rationally. Everyone thus wants more primary goods rather than less.

13. Fishkin, "Justice and Rationality."

14. I mean, of course, the arguments for average utility and for maximin (or, on my construction, a guaranteed minimum). For the former, see note 9 to this chapter.

15. The problem of justice, on Rawls's account, is really the problem of choosing a "basic structure" of society. But the crucial fact about such a basic structure is whether its institutions are organized so as to distribute primary goods according to the principles of justice. It is this *part* of the problem of justice that concerns us, that is, criteria for choices by the government that will affect a person's interests in actual life (which Rawls considers in terms of shares of primary goods). My criterion of nontyranny is, in this way, parallel to maximin. For just as maximin would prescribe that a government raise the minimum share, the principle of nontyranny would prescribe that a government make nontyrannous choices. For comments on the "basic structure" see Rawls, *Theory of Justice*, pp. 7-11; idem, "The Basic Structure as Subject," *American Philosophical Quarterly* 14, no. 2 (April 1977): 159-65; idem, "A Well-Ordered Society," in *Philosophy, Politics and Society*, 5th ser., ed. Peter Laslett and James Fishkin (Oxford: Basil Blackwell/New Haven, Conn.: Yale University Press, 1979).

16. Rawls, *Theory of Justice*, p. 152.

17. They might choose, in other words, to gamble on being one of those who avoids severe deprivations when *some* severe deprivations are inevitable. Note that the argument from the three features against such probabilistic calculations was that the gamble (on average utility) was not worth *introducing* the risk of disaster. But if every alternative imposes severe deprivations, then there is no way to avoid serious risks. In this case, the principle of insufficient reason might offer a reasonable way of minimizing the risk of disaster (by minimizing the number of severe deprivations when some are unavoidable). I mention this only as one way in which agents in the original position might choose to supplement the principle of nontyranny. Whether or not they would, my main argument is unaffected.

18. By the "problem of justice" here I mean the problem of what principle for social choice solves the "priority problem" in Rawls's sense. See note 1 to this chapter.

19. Rawls, *Theory of Justice*, p. 62.

20. Ibid., pp. 302-3.

21. Ibid., p. 63.

22. Ibid., p. 408.

23. Ibid., p. 412.

24. Ibid., p. 409.

25. Ibid., p. 408, n. 11.

26. Ibid., p. 423.

27. Ibid., p. 432.

28. Ibid., p. 73.

29. Ibid.

30. Ibid., p. 74.

31. Ibid., p. 93.

32. Ibid., p. 421.

33. Ibid., p. 143.

Chapter 14

1. This is, of course, the alternative that Rawls calls "intuitionism." See John Rawls, *A Theory of Justice* (Cambridge: Harvard University Press, 1971), section 7.

2. John Stuart Mill, *On Liberty* (New York: Bobbs-Merrill, 1956), p. 13.

3. See, for example, Richard Taylor, *Freedom, Anarchy and the Law* (Englewood Cliffs, N.J.: Prentice-Hall, 1973), pp. 55-60.

4. For an excellent discussion of the range of consequences that might reasonably be included under the notion of "harms," see Joel Feinberg, *Social Philosophy* (Englewood Cliffs, N.J.: Prentice-Hall, 1973), pp. 25-31.

5. I am using two distinguishable notions of "prevent" in this comparison: (1) harm to B is "prevented" if person A is interfered with so that he does not perform an (other-regarding) act that would harm B; (2) harm to B is "prevented" if a government policy connected to that harm is not chosen (in favor of some other policy).

Appendix A

1. I am indebted to Brian Barry and Douglas Rae for the suggestion that I distinguish these two versions of the argument.

2. It should be evident that situations are possible where severe deprivations in the narrow sense are imposed by every alternative. Suppose X's opportunities for a more adequate life chance conflict with Y's (and they could both be satisfied only if some other person were harmed). Our plague example offers a parallel case for subsistence needs. Someone's survival is placed at risk by every alternative in that situation. Every alternative would, therefore, be absolutely ruled out by an absolute rights theory. The result is a blind alley.

3. To see the difficulties in the narrow interpretation consider the following two examples: (a) A policy imposing severe deprivations in the sense of essential interests *not* covered by the narrow view. If a policy would destroy, beyond all recompense, a person's entire life plan and alternative policies would not have harmed anyone, should it not count as tyranny to choose the destructive policy? (b) A choice between one policy imposing severe deprivations in the narrow sense and others imposing them only in the other, want-regarding sense. Are we so confident that, in every case, choice of the first policy must be ruled out? Are there not cases in which the harms resulting from the second policy might be just as bad—or even worse? It is because I am confident about the comparison in (a) and uncertain about the comparison in (b) that I believe the full interpretation to be more defensible.

Appendix B

1. I am indebted to my colleague Douglas Rae for the suggestion that diagrams would clarify this point.

Appendix C

1. John Rawls, *A Theory of Justice* (Cambridge: Harvard University Press, 1971), p. 73.

2. Ibid.

3. Ibid.

4. Ibid., p. 74.

5. I do not mean to imply here that Rawls's formulation of equal opportunity is necessarily inadequate. There are deep problems in determining how far there should be an equalization in the opportunity to *acquire* skills and motivation so as to qualify for equal treatment. Note the effects on the family of any such attempt at equalization. For a critique of notions of equal opportunity that would require more than Rawls's in this respect, see Bernard Williams, "The Idea of Equality," in *Philosophy, Politics and Society,* 2nd ser., ed. Peter Laslett and W.G. Runciman (Oxford: Basil Blackwell, 1962).

Index

The Johns Hopkins University Press

This book was composed in Alphatype Times Roman text and display type by David Lorton from a design by Susan Bishop. It was printed and bound by The Maple Press Company.

Library of Congress Cataloging in Publication Data

Fishkin, James S.
Tyranny and legitimacy.

Expanded and rev. version of the author's contribution to the fifth volume of Philosophy, politics, and society.
Includes index.
1. Political ethics. 2. Legitimacy of governments. 3. Despotism. 4. Social choice. I. Title.
JA79.F57   172   79-11177

ISBN 0-8018-2206-8
ISBN 0-8018-2256-4 (pbk.)

4362 99